Neighborhood Organizing
for
Urban School Reform

Neighborhood Organizing
for
Urban School Reform

Michael R. Williams

Teachers College, Columbia University
New York and London

Published by Teachers College Press, 1234 Amsterdam Avenue,
New York, NY 10027

Copyright © 1989 by Teachers College, Columbia University

Library of Congress Cataloging-in-Publication Data

Williams, Michael R., 1938–
   Neighborhood organizing for urban school reform / Michael R.
Williams.
     p.   cm.
   Bibliography: p.
   Includes index.
   ISBN 0-8077-2931-0.   ISBN 0-8077-2930-2 (pbk.)
   1. Community and school—United States.   2. Education, Urban—
United States.   3. Neighborhood—United States.   I. Title.
LC221.W55   1989   88-29439
370.19'31'0973—dc19   CIP

ISBN 0-8077-2931-0
ISBN 0-8077-2930-2 (paper)

Manufactured in the United States of America

95 94 93 92 91 90 89   1 2 3 4 5 6

For my parents
David Wynn Williams, Jr. and
Florence Ronan Williams

Contents

Acknowledgments   ix

Introduction   1

1. Reassessing the Declining Urban Neighborhood   5

2. Reassessing Victimhood   15

3. The Failures of Inner-City Public Schools   29

4. The Limits of Popular Reform Models   51

5. Forerunners of Citizen Influence in Education   70

6. The Liberal Legacy of Citizen Participation in Education   82

7. Multi-Issue Neighborhood Organizations   102

8. Exploring Organizational Linkages Between Neighborhood and School   116

9. Lessons from Case Studies of Organizing   132

10. Mounting the Campaign to Improve the Neighborhood School   148

Notes   165

References   168

Index   175

About the Author   182

Acknowledgments

Many people have helped shape this work. Technical help came from Aquinas College's Learning Resource Center, its Academic Computing Center, and its sabbatical leave program, which granted me time during the 1985–86 school year to work on this book.

In Milwaukee from 1968 to 1974, the public high school students I taught introduced me to the realities of urban education. Mary Coon, one of the finest teachers I have known, showed me ways to meet the challenges they presented. Later during this period, I struggled along with some special people to create the Highland Community School. They included (but were not limited to) Mike Bolger, Millie Deanes, Cam Derks, Tim Duax, Steve Merkel, Cathy and Frank Miller, Sue Mroczinski, Anne Nephew, Sara Spence, Tim and Angel Souers, and Mary Pat Rose and Don Wallace.

I could never list all the people in Grand Rapids active in its neighborhood organizations who have taught me about the power as well as the frailties of these collective action groups. Concerned public school people here who, I know, have agonized over the disproportionate failure of minority and low-income children *and* have done something about it include Russ Harmelink, Jim Swanlund, the late Sylvester Jones, and a score of teachers in the Grand Rapids schools.

The bibliography lists those authors who have influenced this work, but I am most indebted to my spouse, Mary Alice, who has continually reminded me that the education of children—our own and those of others—is among the most worthwhile of life's works. Our daughters, Christa and Cara, have blossomed because of this belief, convincing me daily of its truth.

Introduction

Few institutions in American society call forth the depths of emotion from us that schools do. Because they embody our noblest aspirations for our youth and our future, they evoke outrage more readily than almost any other institution when they fail. The widespread failure of urban schools is largely their own fault, but this breakdown cannot be understood outside the context of declining neighborhoods and school system bureaucracies, sustained by societal values of race and class separateness.

This book analyzes the barriers citizens meet in organizing to change their schools. Yet these obstacles are not insuperable. I have taught in and studied urban schools; I even helped create one. I also have twenty years' experience with neighborhood organizations, which led me to explore their potential for reforming urban schools.

Community control is a dead issue, if indeed it was ever alive. Rather, this work argues that citizens, especially parents, should be intimately involved in the governance of their children's schools. That is the goal. The strategy to accomplish it, rooted in a long history of citizen participation in education, is for parents to employ the organizational base of their neighborhood or community association to demand voice in the school's operational decision making.

Can poor neighborhoods produce and support viable neighborhood organizations? It is becoming fashionable for scholars to be cynical about the potency of low-to-moderate income neighborhoods to bring off successful long-term organizing. For example, Reginald G. Damerell (1985), departing significantly from his caustic attack on teacher training institutions, claimed that Asian children, one minority, have become ten times as successful as black children, another minority, in New York's public schools. In a similar vein, Nicholas Lemann (1986), writing in *The Atlantic Monthly*, asserted that the "new" ghettos of Chicago are peopled by former sharecroppers from Mississippi and other southern states, who brought with them their dependent ways and inability to cope with the big city. Their neighborhoods, he wrote, are now overpopulated by youths conscripted into gangs and underpopulated by the working-class and middle-class adults of whom a strong social fabric is woven.

Thus, according to the ascendant conservative scholarship, neighborhoods that are inhabited mostly by blacks whose recent roots stretch back to the South are unorganizable and are dominated by prisoners of a world view that avoids intellectual competition, that is not achievement oriented, and that perpetuates the poverty cycle. Blaming-the-victim and culture-of-poverty hypotheses seem to be back in the saddle again.

This book does not deny the social pathology in America's cities. Nor does it naively claim that neighborhood organizations can go it alone in reforming schools; they need a great deal of help from many quarters. Rather, it tries to lay bare the complexities that cause urban schools to fail, as a precondition for organizing. It assumes that the potential for change exists in most low-to-moderate-income neighborhoods in the form of residents, unbeaten by poverty, who can band together to demand improvement in their schools. This assumption is warranted by the presence in most of these neighborhoods of leaders and organizations already at work on neighborhood problems (Boyte, 1980; Hallman, 1984; Williams, 1985).

Given a viable neighborhood organization, can the next step be taken? Can nonprofessionals generate a working relationship with professionals from a starting point of tension or hostility? The paucity of successful examples does not imply that such a partnership cannot be developed. A governance partnership can be developed, but it requires skill and staying power by neighborhood people and considerable help from powerful third parties.

Reform is a political word for a political reality. Any scheme for school improvement that does not include all the actors' interests, especially their need for some control over the outcomes, is a sham. This book is written under that assumption, and with the fervent hope that the lessons learned from the neighborhood organizing of the past four decades can be brought to bear upon the problems of schools.

Chapter 1 discusses the sources of urban decline in terms of a structural relationship between haves and have-nots, Saul Alinsky's names for those whom social scientists have labeled the advantaged and disadvantaged of American society. This structural relationship is *prejudice* as it finds form in the rules and regulations, practices and procedures of American institutions, from the national government to local municipalities, from multinational corporations and banks to mom-and-pop stores, from great universities to local elementary schools. Yet this separating mechanism is not just impersonal; individuals personally maintain it. In the light of this structural relationship, the chapter reassesses the urban low-income neighborhood as a setting for political organizing, concluding on the basis of past studies that organizing in such poor neighborhoods is more likely to emphasize the political dimension rather than community building, precisely because of the desperate need of the residents and their alienation from the "establishment."

Chapter 2 explores resident attitudes toward schools found in poor neighborhoods. Attitudes of self-blame by poor people, feelings that they have no control over their lives, have been documented and analyzed for years. How the local school promotes and reinforces these feelings in students and parents receives further clarification, however. Nonetheless, other poor residents, channeling their fury at their oppressors, succeed in rearing offspring who can compete in a hostile white world; these residents form a leadership pool for organizing.

Chapter 3 is a brief analysis of the complexity of the schooling process, from classroom to district level, which obscures the operation of institutional racism and class prejudice. The culture shock experienced by white middle-class teachers and nonwhite working-class youth alike leads to overreaction and lowered expectations for student achievement. In addition, too many teachers are technically inadequate in their teaching of skills and subject matter; this instructional inadequacy is greatly magnified in the inner-city school. The machine-like characteristics of the school system still enthrall educators and public alike, causing much of the recent reform literature to focus too much on improved efficiency and not enough on the organic aspects of school systems that would promote greater participation by citizens, especially parents and students, in the operation of their schools.

Chapter 4 compares and contrasts several recently proposed models of school reform, both in terms of their conceptualization of the problem of school failure and of how change will occur. These models include packaged curriculum innovations, the excellent corporation model of Peters and Waterman, the partnership model of David Seeley, the third-party intervention model suggested by James Comer, and the creation of collaborative site-governance groups proposed by Bruce Joyce and his associates. The chapter concludes that Joyce's proposed structure is appropriate, but the remaining six chapters of the book are devoted to an analysis of how the neighborhood organization can achieve it.

Chapters 5 and 6 form a tandem historical review of citizen participation in American public schools for the past century and a half. Chapter 5 brings readers up to the 1960s through the rise of the rigid school bureaucracy of the late 1800s and its subsequent loosening under the liberal-progressive reforms of the early twentieth century, which saw the beginning of the social work approach to organizing the poor. Labor organizing before and during the Great Depression was the backdrop for the emergence of Saul Alinsky, whose legacy of radical community organizing informs today's neighborhood organizing movement. Chapter 6 adds an analysis of federal initiatives in urban renewal that has spurred a variety of forms of citizen participation in educational decision making.

Chapter 7 examines the contemporary neighborhood organization itself: its leaders, membership, motivations, goals, issues, norms, and group evolution. The chapter concludes that these multi-issue organizations are superior to single-issue parent groups as instruments for reforming the local school. Chapter 8 critically explores theoretical linking mechanisms between neighborhood and school. Most mechanisms proposed in the literature focus on the individual actor, beginning with the isolated parent complaining to the teacher, but what is needed is a strong organization (a collective mechanism) if school policy is to be influenced by the community. Chapter 9, therefore, presents case studies of neighborhood organizing for urban school reform in order to draw lessons common to them. And Chapter 10 concludes the book with a specific set of suggestions and considerations for neighborhood organizations oriented toward improving their local school.

Though much of this advice is well grounded both in the literature of school politics and organizing and in my own experience, it is too general, which implies a shortcoming, because in organizing, context is everything. In addition, there are precious few recorded examples of success in this endeavor. Keeping these facts in mind, I would appreciate contact with any reader who has experience with this process of neighborhood organizing for urban school reform, whether it be judged successful or a failure. (My mailing address is Aquinas College, Grand Rapids, Michigan 49506.)

1

Reassessing the Declining Urban Neighborhood

What white Americans have never fully understood—but what the negro can never forget—is that white society is deeply implicated in the ghetto. White institutions created it, white institutions maintain it, and white society condones it. (Report, 1968, p. 2)

Urban decline has two meanings. The first is descriptive, which means the loss of jobs and people. The second is functional and refers to socially undesirable changes that reduce the ability of a city to perform its social functions effectively. In other words, as city life deteriorates in quality, unpleasantness, social problems, and crime all increase. In an extensive analysis of 153 of the nation's largest cities, Katherine Bradbury, Anthony Downs, and Kenneth Small (1982) tested several dozen theories of decline. They concluded that (1) race discrimination has played an active role in suburbanization—the more blacks became concentrated in the central city, the more rapid was suburban growth; and (2) economic opportunity in the suburbs lured firms and people to leave the city behind. Racial bias and economic considerations have thus been a one-two punch to the midsection of the central city. Sixty-three percent of these cities were either barely maintaining a balance or were losing people and jobs to the suburbs.

THE SOURCES OF URBAN DECLINE

Decline is not a neutral word. Race and class antagonisms are at the heart of urban decline, held in place and even exacerbated by the ways social institutions are structured. Socioeconomic systems reinforce these divisions by their very function, though how they do this is not immediately apparent. For our purposes, one of their major consequences is that these systems combine to withdraw capital from certain parts of the city.

Capital is represented by money. A "built environment," such as a neighborhood, needed money to be built and needs money to maintain itself. The first event is investment, the second reinvestment. Quite simply, unless the neighborhoods where the schools under discussion are located receive a regular infusion of reinvestment, they will continue to decay. This reinvestment means not only money in the form of loans for rehabilitating old buildings but also money to create new businesses or expand older ones so that employment opportunities are opened up for residents, and the goods and services they require become more readily available.

American capitalism encourages investment to be directed to areas where it will receive the highest rate of return. Such a principle appears grounded in common sense, but it carries grave long-term social consequences. For example, it might mean moving a factory out of a city to a suburb, further eroding the city's tax base (which is a major source of support for the schools). Or a northern factory may relocate in the South, aggravating the already higher unemployment rates in the Frostbelt. Or the multinational corporation may decide to rebuild in a foreign country where labor costs are lower, putting even more competitive pressure on home-built products. In another vein, lenders may decide to boycott lending for more small business purchase or maintenance in inner cities because they can obtain better returns on their loans in suburban districts. Insurers, too, often refuse to cover buildings or businesses in the inner city, thus putting added pressure on anyone entertaining the idea of investment there.

Not all investment is healthy for the inner-city neighborhood, however. There are certain types of investors who seek short-term gain in these communities by buying old housing cheaply and renting to low-income tenants without maintaining the properties. Whatever the difficulties these speculators encounter, they will not lose money, because they can either unload the properties for more than they paid or get considerable tax advantages by claiming large losses. Other speculators may buy and resell properties many times over to inflate their prices, then burn them for the insurance money.

Let us not lose track of the main point. It does not matter whether one pictures bankers as helpless in the face of low inner-city demand for loans, or speculators as malevolent capitalist pigs: The main reason that neighborhoods decline is that they are not nourished by an adequate supply of capital, and decisions not to nourish are made by those institutions that control capital.

The federal government has been another major diverter of capital from the inner city, particularly in its policies that favor the shift of capital from the Frostbelt to the Sunbelt (Morris, 1980). It has accomplished this dislocation by moving 300,000 federal government jobs to the Sunbelt, granting a disproportionate share of defense contracts there, and failing to make cost-of-living allowances in Social Security and other entitlements for the higher cost of living in the North. These phenomena have gone largely unnoticed by the public, whose attention has focused on federal grants to cities. Although these block grants have been aimed at rebuilding crumbling urban centers, they have increasingly propped up ailing city budgets in the past two decades. Frostbelt cities particularly have become like welfare recipients, dependent on the federal dole to get by. The Reagan administration appeared to set as one of its main priorities the blocking of this pipeline to cities so as to redirect funds into a military buildup.

The cycle of urban decline, thus set in motion, is kept in motion. Jobs and people leave the city. Those remaining behind are less able collectively to support the maintenance of city services. So taxes must be increased, in turn prompting further exodus.

American capitalism may provide contradictory incentives both to invest in and to plunder the urban landscape; the federal government may offer its own variety of skewed incentives for the maldistribution of capital, but urban institutions also embody sources of breakdown (Winner, 1977). The urban resident constantly encounters the effects of large, complex organizations, technological feats that undergird modern urban life. Yet these organizations seem ungovernable, carrying their own technological imperatives to control their human controllers. This analysis of "technology out of control" parallels our own commonsense feeling of being at the mercy of systems: government, business, social services, schools. While urban systems are not things in themselves, their very size and complexity seem to block even organized attempts at change. Since we should not underestimate the tendencies of large human organizations to subordinate their human agents to what seem to be their own ends, we will return to analyze the urban school system in a later chapter.

Analysis of urban decline would be incomplete without attention to the role that perception plays in it. When citizens have perceived that an area is in trouble, whether because of the physical deterioration or the increasing numbers of "undesirable persons" in it, they have often reacted in ways that pushed it further toward decline. They sold out and fled, or if they stayed, they deferred maintenance on their properties. Many retained ownership but rented to more transient occupants. Perception's role in neighborhood decline and revitalization has been fully analyzed elsewhere (Goetze, 1979); it is sufficient to note here that it is a major ingredient not only in urban decline but also in urban revitalization. If a neighborhood or a city is to be reborn, its residents must hope that improvement is occurring and will continue. Creating the reasonable expectation of a better common future is a principal goal of the urban neighborhood organization.

In summary, the structure of urban decline is grounded in the contradictions of capitalism and the government that serves it. Complex organization masks these contradictions even as it does violence to those it purports to serve. Resident perceptions that decline is inevitable lead to behaviors that further hasten deterioration.

This explanation seems to clash with the commonsense notion that neighborhoods in trouble are so because they are overloaded with people who are less able to contribute to the development of the area. They may be the mentally ill, left to roam the streets when their former institutions were shut down in the deinstitutionalization movement; rural immigrants, unskilled and unable to find work; or merely the old, left behind in homes they had occupied for decades as the neighborhood changed. It is the human problems that gain the public's attention, but concentrations of problem persons are the result of a neighborhood's being left to die by powerful outside forces, not its cause. Withdrawal of capital is the actual cause of decline. Race and class antagonisms are the life and breath behind these institutional decisions. These attitudes, the decisions they provoke, and the resultant distribution of wealth and opportunity constitute the structural relationship between haves and have-nots in our society.

THE DISTRESSED NEIGHBORHOOD
AS A CONTEXT FOR ORGANIZING

An Initial Description of Decline

People often equate central city with inner city, and frequently use these terms interchangeably with "the poor section of town," the ghetto, the black community, the slums, and so forth. To avoid confusion, throughout this book, *central city* will refer to the entire geographic area governed by the largest municipality (usually centrally located in the Standard Metropolitan Statistical Area—roughly, the metropolitan area). The *inner city* will refer to all census tracts within the central city whose median household income is below the median for the city. Often, but not always, these areas are disproportionately populated by minority residents. They are virtually always characterized by larger-than-normal numbers of aging and deteriorated or abandoned buildings and by a general dreariness. They are not necessarily more densely populated than any other area of the city (measured by the number of people per square mile), but their living units are more likely to be overcrowded (the number of people per room). As an example, Chicago in its entirety is a central city; its West Side is an inner city. Declining neighborhoods are, for the most part, in the inner city, although they are also found in older suburbs.

Types of Neighborhoods

Scholars have typified neighborhoods in many ways. Anthony Downs (1981), for example, described them by stages of deterioration, but this approach gives little insight into the sources of resurgence they may contain. Sandra Schoenberg and Patricia Rosenbaum (1980), on the other hand, classified neighborhoods according to their *viability*, or residents' potential to control the social order. This concept of viability borrows from other studies of neighborhood types and builds on the notion of internal and external networking (Warren & Warren, 1977). Viability requires four elements:

1. Resident agreement on public behavior
2. Development of an organizational network
3. Creation of linkages to outside economic and political resources
4. Internal exchange relationships to resolve conflict

The most viable neighborhood is the one which most residents identify with, a place wherein they interact with one another, and beyond whose borders they maintain many social, political, and economic ties.

Neighborhoods can be classified along a continuum of each variable. Although the distressed neighborhood rates lower than the most viable neighborhood, it should not be written off. Many of its residents do identify with it, do interact with one another (increasingly through neighborhood organizations and block clubs), and do maintain ties beyond its borders.

Neighborhood as a Political Concept

This work argues that troubled urban neighborhoods not only contain those "meaningful communities" and leaders that are essential for school reform but also that their neighborhood organizations are political; that is, they are organized primarily for political purposes rather than for building community. Though not all distressed neighborhoods are organized, many are or could be, and through these organizations, the forces of blight that infest the communities could be grappled with. A brief overview of the evolution of the concept of *neighborhood* during the past century should begin to reveal the differences between it and *community*.

There have been two periods in which neighborhood appears to have been the dominant unit of analysis in thinking about cities (Miller, 1981). Between 1880 and 1920, when cities reached a new peak in immigration and industrial energy, observers saw them as clusters of interlacing communities. Neighborhood and community appeared to merge. But with the corruption of ward-based municipal government, reformers pushed successfully for nonpartisan elections, professional management, and civil service examinations as the prerequisite for government jobs. The complex, nearly ungovernable mosaic of nationalities, races, and classes led theorists to focus on either the urban individual or the metropolis itself as the basic unit of analysis and to abandon the possibility of creating community within cities.

The period following World War I thus became the era of "Community Lost" to those social scientists who implicitly equated neighborhood with community (Wellman & Leighton, 1979). Community Lost asserted that the bureaucratic nature of urban society so weakened primary ties that most individuals were driven to depend on formal organizations, such as the military, the church, the firm, or the university, as the principal community. Based on the assumption that people are easily corruptible, if not fundamentally evil, this view emphasized social disorganization. It implied that as the proportion of low-to-moderate-income residents in a typical urban neighborhood increases, these people experience isolation, privatization, alienation, and despair. As the constraints of communal structures vanish, these unfortunates turn to robbery, rape, and riot.

Since World War II, however, many social scientists have reemphasized the neighborhood as a basic unit of analysis. One branch of research found massive evidence of community within urban neighborhoods. "Community Saved" saw the linkages between people as ideally most dense within the neighborhood boundaries and found evidence to this effect in many such regions of America's cities after 1945. Both Community Lost and Community Saved perspectives admitted, in their tendency to equate neighborhood with community, that there may be external linkages across neighborhood boundaries, but they stressed that these personal connections are fewer and weaker than those within the borders.

A second postwar branch of research examined the "Community of Limited Liability." According to this concept, individuals within a geographic neighborhood established many ties and commitments to communities outside its boundaries, such as churches, fraternal and labor organizations, and even family networks. These neighborhood residents could still interact locally with each other, but the individual was only partially interconnected with others. His or her social needs could be fulfilled either inside or outside the neighborhood's borders. This concept of overlapping communities was a more sophisticated one than its more extreme cousin, "Community Liberated," which asserted that in many urban areas the strongest bonds and links are beyond neighborhood borders. Networks, according to this model, branched out in unpredictable ways, but they were not rooted in the neighborhood. This form of networking was to be distinguished from the sparse networks of Community Lost and the dense networks of Community Saved, both within the borders.

The late 1960s saw a breakdown of faith in urban community as a way to meet one's social and economic needs. Community, at this point, still seemed to be synonymous with neighborhood; it now shifted to mean homogeneous interest groups: blacks, ethnics, women, gays, the aged. Separatism and advocacy became the watchwords.

What does this analysis tell us about the relationship between neighborhood and community? Certainly for most urban dwellers, neighborhood currently implies both the social sense of community and the political sense derived from geographic location. Neighborhoods are the setting for the social functions of neighboring: informal interaction and influence, provision for help in need or emergency, and the occasion for local pride and status giving. In the distressed neighborhood, the neighborhood is also the setting for organizing, which is a political act rooted in concern about neighborhood conditions, feelings of threat, a sense of identification with the area, and a degree of optimism about the residents' ability to control the social fabric (Williams, 1985). The following study highlights how the contemporary urban neighborhood is more likely a political phenomenon than a community.

From Community Organizations to Neighborhood Organizations

Barrett Lee and associates (1984) assessed changes in the neighborhood organizations of Seattle, Washington, from 1929 to 1979.

Their objective was to test the hypothesis that neighborhoods are essentially natural communities or places primarily of social or neighborly interaction. They suspected, of course, that this natural community thesis might be simplistic in that it ignored the political aspect of neighborhood life.

Assuming that neighborhood organizations would probably show evidence of community, they defined neighborhood organizations as "indigenously formed voluntary associations of residents dedicated to maintaining or improving conditions within a restricted geographical area" (p. 1164). They compared 60 neighborhood organizations of 1929 with 74 such groups in 1979, whose turfs were, for the most part, coextensive. The authors proposed five hypotheses, the first two of which they called "functional" and the latter three "participational." The main functional hypothesis was that resident participation, over time, would have changed from *social* ("providing a chance to get together informally") to *political* ("seeking to improve or maintain the current character of the area") (p. 1181, n. 14). The second, by implication, was that coalition building among these groups would have progressed from rare to common. Participational hypotheses were that resident involvement would have shifted from extensive to limited, membership requirements from restrictive to open, and membership composition from homogeneous to heterogeneous. For simplicity's sake we will consider the participational hypotheses first.

Data analysis indicated that resident involvement had indeed become more limited. The 1929 groups met more frequently and hosted many more social events; in fact, 23 of the 60 groups owned their own community clubhouses and regularly sponsored dinner dances. Membership in the early groups was effectively restricted to white homeowners, requiring formal application and admission by majority vote of members with final approval by the governing board. Five decades later, after the neighborhoods had become much more diverse, membership was more easily attainable. All one had to do was show up at meetings and, where required, pay dues. It goes almost without saying that the membership shifted over these years from homogeneous to heterogeneous. But the 1979 survey indicated that, although nonwhites, younger persons, or renters were represented on nearly half the governing boards, they still tended to be dominated by white middle-aged homeowners.

The functional hypotheses, our main concern in this work, were not so simply confirmed. There was an actual shift from social to political emphasis over the fifty-year period, but other historical sources indicated that the early neighborhood organizations took root and grew in response to an amendment in Seattle's city charter, which transformed the election of city councilpersons from a ward to an at-large basis, a change which undermined the geographic representation the neighborhoods had previously enjoyed. The neighborhood organizations came into existence to continue resident political pressure for provision of public services. This unexpected finding only serves to underscore the point that neighborhood organizations are essentially political in nature.

Earlier neighborhood organizations were also able to build coalitions more easily than their modern counterparts because of the similarity of their concerns. They were much less likely within a federation to see winners and losers among their number than would federations of contemporary neighborhoods so different in racial and ethnic composition and in income.

The central conclusion reached by the authors was that the decline-of-community thesis, which rests on the assumption that neighborhoods are communities, fails to give primacy to the political nature of neighborhoods. Neighborhoods have always been sites of economic investment and, therefore, of political interests. A limited community view, which allows attention to both political and social aspects of neighborhood, is a more accurate approach and casts doubt on a supposed golden age of the American neighborhood and its subsequent decline.

CONCLUSION

Although haves create and maintain the have-not neighborhoods by exerting a myriad of discriminatory pressures through their institutions as well as their individual decisions, these inner-city neighborhoods are not the urban wastelands that the media stereotypically project. It is true that many of them suffer inordinate rates of social pathology, but they contain many strong individuals, families, and social networks.

The search for community in these neighborhoods may be misled by two false assumptions. The first is that neighborhood and community are synonymous. The second is that without such a solidaristic or comprehensive community basis, collective political action is impossible. The ordinary forms of community, that is, communities based on kin, church, or other ties, do exist in these communities as primary forms of linkage. In fact, Community Saved is more prevalent than Community Lost because, lacking many (but certainly not all) external ties because of lack of transportation or race discrimination, these residents are likely to form internal ties in order to conserve, control, and efficiently pool their meager resources.

The organizations that develop in these neighborhoods will be political in nature (Lamb, 1975). Those who focus on organizing as an activity whose main goal is to create community or cohesion within the neighborhood's borders are prone to employ strategies that avoid conflict with institutions. The Settlement House movement of 1895–1915 and the School-as-Community-Center movement spreading over the first half of this century are examples of such community organizing that fell into a social work approach to solving problems of the neighborhood.

I have used the term neighborhood instead of community as the modifier of organizing to emphasize the political nature of this activity. Organizing may enhance community, but its principal goal is the improvement of neighborhood conditions, in this case, the neighborhood school. Later chapters describe the characteristics of neighborhood organizations and the tactics they may employ with schools.

Our investigation of the school problem, however, is far from complete. In the next chapter, we analyze the criticism made by even well-intentioned educators that the source of low have-not academic achievement still remains in the have-not neighborhood—even admitting that its condition is the result of the discrimination and oppression by have society. This is the complaint that the students (and by implication their parents) have become functionally inferior, unable psychologically to perform to middle-class standards, a beaten class of people whose experience of failure is so profound as to deprive them of motivation. Hence, so the argument goes, there is no point to inner-city school reform.

2

Reassessing Victimhood

Today educational sociologists paint a more complex picture wherein the school mediates family background, and educational outcomes are affected by a combination of school actions, family background, and student actions, in the context of educational environments. (Borman & Spring, 1984, p. 2)

This book takes the position that schools are primarily responsible for the low academic achievement of inner-city youth. But there is an interactive effect between school processes and the attitudes and behaviors of their charges and parents. Not only do the schools not work at educating these students, but they then tell the students in a variety of direct and indirect ways that they themselves are to blame for their own failure. It is not surprising that many students come to expect little of themselves. This process of accommodation by both sides is central to an understanding of urban school failure; it is also a major obstacle to organizing for school reform.

This chapter, therefore, examines more precisely how it is that many of the victims of school oppression become unwitting coconspirators, as it were, in their own failure. Many parents and their children, it should quickly be noted, steadfastly refuse to blame themselves and rightly focus their fury on the school, though all too often this anger is diffused and held back because it is unorganized. The chapter begins with an analysis of theories that have been used to place some or all of the blame on these children, their families, their neighborhoods, or their subcultures. The chapter than reviews an important study of the failure process in an inner-city neighborhood before discussing studies of parent interaction with their children, learned helplessness, and stigmatization. It concludes with implications of this work for organizing the neighborhood to improve its schools.

INACCURATE THEORIES OF FAILURE

The structural relationship between the advantaged and the disadvantaged sectors of society has partly been maintained by a variety of theories that distract from an accurate understanding of the problem. These theories fall into two clusters: theories that deny such a relationship between haves and have-nots and theories that affirm such a relationship but pose it in stark, simplistic, or ideological terms (Payne, 1984). The first are denial theories; the second, progressive theories. The first group blames the victims; the second blames society while romanticizing the victims.

Denial Theories

Attribute Theories. Among the denial theories, attribute theories are the most common; they find the cause of the plight of the poor within the poor themselves; that is, some internal attribute or characteristic holds them in poverty. One view, not currently fashionable, is that minority children are genetically inferior as a group.[1] Another, more popular hypothesis is that they are functionally inferior because of poor self-concept, family background, or even their relationship with their past ("Blacks came out of slavery, so they could not be expected to compete on an equal basis with whites!"). The well-known culture of poverty hypothesis also purports to describe functional inferiority. Ghetto children's language differences are not just differences but evidence of inadequacy if not retardation. They lack a middle-class school orientation, it is said, which presumably means unwillingness or inability to comply with the school's behavioral expectations, such as obedience to school authority or application to assigned tasks. A great deal of criticism has been written against these attribute theories, which need not be repeated here. Suffice it to say that they are simplistic at best, racist at worst.

Opportunity Theories. These theories are a more subtle category of denial. They find that inequitable distribution of wealth is a cause of the have-nots' desperate condition, but somehow this maldistribution is not caused by haves. It is simply a given—the way things are. At bottom, this view is a conservative acceptance of the status quo as inevitable, given the imperatives of scarce resources and competition for them. Neither attribute nor opportunity theories acknowledge that there is a causal relationship between haves and have-nots that must be continually maintained by socal institutions and cultural mores.

Other forms of denial theory do admit to some relationship between the two social spheres but trivialize or misjudge it.

Mysticism.   This theory is called mysticism because it relies on vague moralistic or subjective explanations that reduce racial or class relations to people's interpersonal attitudes. According to this theory, what is wrong is that these attitudes are prejudiced; justice, then, can be achieved by correcting these prejudices. This analysis is patently superficial, for it does not deal with how these attitudes have become enmeshed in institutions.

RAP Thesis.   Another form of denial is the "Redneck-as-Patsy," or RAP thesis. Here the relationship is couched in terms of the antagonism between those of slightly higher socioeconomic status than the poor and the poor themselves. These have-a-little-want-mores are the true exploiters of the poor, not the higher classes, according to this view. The further one is removed from poverty, the less one should be subjected to scrutiny as a cause of poverty. In the case of inner-city schools, these "rednecks" would be the teachers. Both of these latter explanations, mysticism and RAP, encourage a good person/bad person view of social issues. All four deny a structural interaction between haves and have-nots.

Progressive Theories

This group of explanations stands denial theories on their collective head. Now the structural relation is everything and suddenly the poor become what the rich have made them. They are only the sum of their oppression. For example, William Ryan's (1971) classic polemic, *Blaming the Victim*, is an impassioned defense of the poor against the myriad slanders of the many forms of denial theories. Yet Ryan seems not to allow the poor any responsibility for playing out their lives, a well-meaning oversight that robs them of the potential to take back some control over their lives.

A recent criticism of English and American urban schools has been grounded in neo-Marxian theory: not only do conflicts between groups over resources give rise to school problems, but the great contradiction of capitalism itself—the lust for profit versus the social costs of maximizing it—is the root of urban educational failure (Grace, 1984). This ideological perspective makes the structural relationship a thing in itself, whereby the very directions of societal interaction are predetermined. It does not matter whether one focuses on the present and past victories of capital over social benefit or on the synthesis that is to arise after the capitalist victory is too complete and social benefit is crushed. Again, ideology removes from the picture the possibility of individuals working collectively in ways other than violent revolution to create outcomes other than those predicted by the theory.

An adequate theory of failure, then, must allow a paradox. On the one hand, there is a class struggle—the structural relationship between haves and have-nots—although it is masked by the affluence of American society and by a social process called fragmentation. On the other hand, many members of the working classes and many minorities adapt to their oppression in ways that only hurt themselves.

FRAGMENTATION

Fragmentation, a term originated by Max Weber, arises from the complexity of the social process of modern industrial societies. That is, the relationships among the many actors and institutions that result in a social problem are so complex that the process is not seen at all. Charles Payne (1984), a sophisticated observer of urban education, provides an example of how a black child born in poverty is pushed into the ranks of the structurally unemployed partly by the schooling process he undergoes. What is remarkable is that no one involved perceives himself or herself as having anything to do with this outcome. In Payne's words, this denial of responsibility is the "rationalization of inequality" (1984, p. 38), made possible by fragmentation.

This child's first-grade teacher decided, let us suppose, that he had little chance to learn because he was poorly dressed, smelled faintly of urine, and spoke in street dialect. So she made little effort to teach him because she had many other duties. Similar judgments were made by later teachers as he was passed along from one grade to another. Later, his sixth-grade teacher found him so far below the appropriate skill levels that he taught him nothing. His high-school counselor advised him, based on his record, to take shop courses. Four years after this, a personnel officer sent him away after a poor performance on an employment test. He joined the U.S. Army, became a combat soldier, and returned to approach other personnel officers some years later, only to find that he had not learned marketable skills as a combat recruit. "You can call the process racist," writes Payne, "but there need be no racists in it. There are no generalists here, only specialists in a process too fragmented to be easily identified as a process" (1984, p. 39).

At this point many inner-city grade-school teachers would rise to claim that many of their charges are indeed not capable of performing "normally" in school. Their cultural experiences have been limited much more than those of middle-class children, they say; their language development is retarded, and so forth. This defensiveness, spoken in terms of denial theories, is born of culture shock, to be sure. It is also grounded in teachers' feelings of inadequacy and isolation, and there probably *are* more children in the inner city with emotional and intellectual deficits.

But all too often, this response is also a denial of responsibility, the "rationalization of inequality." The inner-city school, with the teachers on the front lines, responds to these different children in ways that grossly exaggerate and reinforce their weaknesses. The next chapter addresses how this interaction occurs.

There is thus a broad range of inappropriate theories of inner-city school failure. Fragmentation explains how difficult it is to perceive the process accurately. The following case study of urban school breakdown provides careful data and insight into how the process functions.

A CASE STUDY OF URBAN SCHOOL BREAKDOWN

John Ogbu (1974), a Nigerian-born anthropologist, interviewed hundreds of parents, students, school personnel, and other community members for his study of school-community relationships in a low-income neighborhood, Burgherside (he called it), in Stockton, California, during the late 1970s. He concluded that widespread school failure in that area represented an adaptation by the children to limited opportunities available through education. Although the larger community of taxpayers in Stockton saw the schools as the principal vehicle to economic success, the minority poor were only too aware of the job discrimination that lay ahead for them after school was finished.

The attitudes and behaviors of the various parties Ogbu studied are instructive. Parents, for example, showed a lack of effort by tolerating frequent school absences by their children, although some Hispanics kept their children home on occasion as interpreters. Parents often disciplined their children harshly for grades below C, but they admitted they did not know how to encourage their youngsters. Parental moves of residence, typical in poverty communities, frequently took students from one school to another. Parents did, however, place primary responsibility for their children's academic learning on the schools, a view many middle-class parents would share.

Students also demonstrated self-defeating attitudes and behaviors. For example, they often spoke of their desire to go to college, yet they did not try to take college preparatory courses and talked openly of "settling for" Cs and Ds. They were satisfied with this below-standard achievement because they believed they could not get better grades from their teachers. The pull of the peer group away from academic goals, found in many adolescent subcultures, was heightened in Burgherside, as it often is in inner-city schools. I recall at a hearing in 1984 a black middle-school principal bemoaning the absence of any black students in his honors program, although he estimated that in the five busloads of black students coming daily from the inner city to his affluent neighborhood location, there were at least a dozen capable of qualifying and following through. He testified that whenever black students did begin to attend honors classes, they were taunted unmercifully by their friends on the bus until they resigned. He could think of no solution for this problem. Two years later, in a conversation with the superintendent, I asked if the principal had solved this problem. The superintendent, a man concerned about low minority achievement in his district, responded that he had not but should have, and was therefore removed from his principalship. A later section of this chapter further examines this self-defeating form of student adaptation.

Since Ogbu's study was anthropological in nature, he studied the Burgherside schools' subculture within the context of the set of beliefs and values held by most of Stockton's middle-class residents. Since they were taxpayers, most of them held that the function of school was, in essence, to create more taxpayers. And since disproportionate numbers of Burghersiders were on welfare, the schools were seen as agencies to help them (or their children) enter the taxpayer rolls (though taxpayers gave little thought to the fact of job discrimination). Therefore, schools were staffed by taxpayers (teachers) who acted as social workers to the neighborhood people. The whole relationship of school to poor neighborhood, as taxpayers saw it, was one of clientage, giving rise to great social distance between taxpayers and nontaxpaying community members. In Ogbu's view, virtually all the interactions between teachers and Burghersiders could be explained according to this social work model.

Ogbu observed that most teachers acted as if they believed in the functional inferiority of their students. They believed, more specifically, that

1. parent involvement, as they defined it, would promote student academic success,
2. Burgherside households had no fathers, and that
3. Burghersiders were caught in the welfare cycle.

As to the first belief, Ogbu found that parents saw parental involvement as either frustrating contacts with the school or make-work incidental activities, neither of which had anything to do with their children's learning. The second belief did not take into account that, in fact, nurturing men—usually though not always the fathers—were very much a part of growing children's lives in a poor black neighborhood. Frequently, however, these men did not live in the same household with these children, either because economic security, required for a traditional marriage, was sadly lacking, or because welfare eligibility requirements militated against men in the house. As for the welfare cycle itself, Ogbu's investigation determined that few welfare mothers were second-generation recipients. Their reasons for getting on welfare varied: some lacked knowledge of birth control and in late adolescence found themselves with a child to support; others maintained sexual liaisons with several men in order to support themselves. Few, however, said they wanted to be on welfare.[2]

Taxpayers, strongly convinced of the functional inferiority of these low-income families, saw the schools as agencies of rehabilitation, a missionary effort to save the child from the effects of his or her disorganized family background and bad neighborhood. Programs to meet this end, such as behavior modification and individualized curriculum packages, were introduced into the schools without the advice and consent of the parents. For example, when parents found out that English as a Second Language (ESL) and bilingual programs were being tried in Head Start and early elementary grades, they were upset. They wanted proper English stressed from the beginning. They saw this case as one more instance in which taxpayers viewed them as inferior and incapable of making wise judgments about their children's own best interests. They wanted to be involved in the development of programs that served them because, though the taxpayers (that is, school personnel) may have been well meaning, they did not "think poor."

Parents had several other concerns, which Ogbu listed. First, schools could not change the Burgherside parents or neighborhood, but they could provide the children a quality education. Second, parents feared heightened class consciousness among their children as a result of busing. They wanted quality education in their own neighborhood. Third, most said they did not want "community control" of their schools, but further probing revealed that they felt it could not happen anyway. The overall response theme was more a fatalistic one than an active political rejection of the idea. Fourth, as to school programming, parents thought Head Start was good but thought that all teachers should speak and demand from students correct English. They also contended that the curriculum should reflect the cultures of black and brown people, that it should train for college and jobs, and that student promotion should be based on grade, not age. Finally, parents pleaded for a change in the direction of communication between school and home from one-way to two-way. They felt everything went *from* school *to* parent.

This study reveals almost all the themes important to understanding why urban schools do not work for many children. There is maladaptive behavior on the part of students and parents. There is the set of beliefs by the middle class, especially school personnel, about the functional inferiority of the community members. There is the resulting imposition of programs on the community and its predictable resentment at being treated so paternalistically. This paternalism shows itself, according to other accounts, in a range of educator behaviors that convey to the students and parents that they are functionally inferior (Payne, 1984).

Thus, many inner-city parents and students display self-destructive attitudes toward schools. John Ogbu's view was that their feelings and actions were adaptations to the contradiction between the promise of education as the avenue to economic success, on the one hand, and the reality of school discrimination, wherein Cs were the highest marks given regardless of effort, and job discrimination after graduation, on the other hand. The diagram in Figure 2.1 is my attempt to schematize the process Ogbu discusses.

Ogbu's study showed that parents had many valid and important things to say about their children and about how school should treat them. Yet at the same time, they often did not interact effectively with school personnel. For example, many of Ogbu's parent interviewees seemed to follow this logic:

1. "Teachers think I'm dumb."
2. "Teachers will not accept my opinions about my own children."
3. "If teachers think I'm dumb, then I should stay home."

In other words, instead of stepping up contact with teachers when classroom problems arose, parents reduced the little contact there had been.

FIGURE 2.1

JOHN OGBU'S MODEL OF SCHOOL FAILURE

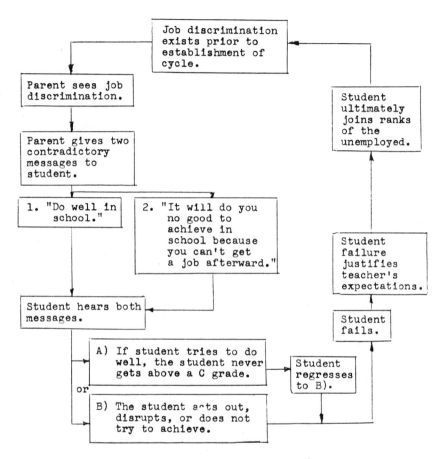

When parents did talk to teachers, they demonstrated other foolish behaviors. Some played the role of victim of a bad neighborhood, the client position that the "social worker/teacher" saw them in. In this way they avoided taking responsibility for a problem they did not "own"— their child's school failure. Other parents did not challenge school inequities out of a sense of fatalism: "How can I change anything here?"

Students, too, showed evidence of fatalism to Ogbu. They blamed their parents more than their teachers for their failures.

Payne's interviews with Chicago's Westside High School students also showed that they did not blame the school for their failure. They responded instead with such comments as, "I'm stupid"; "The teachers here really are nice people"; or "I'm just the victim of [vague] racism" (1984, pp. 148–49).

FURTHER STUDIES ON FATALISM

Sociologist Rodman Webb (1981) reviewed several studies on the phenomenon of learned helplessness in order to gain greater insight into poverty children's school failure. In a controlled experiment with kindergarten children, one group was placed in problem-solving situations where no appropriate strategies seemed available. A second group in the same situations had been trained in appropriate solutions. When possible solutions were suggested or made available, the first group was less able to utilize them effectively; they had learned to be helpless.

In another study, those children who had a good sense that they themselves had a degree of control over the reinforcements they received from the environment (that is, a high *internal locus of control*) did not learn helplessness as readily as those who felt things were out of their control to begin with (a high *external locus of control*). Other studies have documented how teachers in the early grades place certain students at a disadvantage by

1. Blocking their attempts to participate or succeed
2. Withholding reinforcements when they do succeed
3. Sending negative messages
4. Encouraging the rest of the class to participate in stigmatizing them as failures.

These students developed a sense of academic and social isolation. They felt impotent, humiliated, and angry, all of which led to a loss of sense of internal control, to fatalistic behavior, and to low school achievement.

Thus, there is often a reciprocal relationship between the external social and economic environment and the inner-city children's and parents' attitudes about their own control over their lives. Jeff Howard and Ray Hammond (1985) have investigated the hidden obstacles to success for many blacks. They offer a perceptive explanation for the black performance gap on intellectual measures (significantly lower mean scores) from SAT scores to teacher competency examinations. Many blacks, including middle-class blacks, have over the years internalized the feeling that they are intellectually inferior, a message that the larger society has consistently sent them. Their performance problems in intellectual competition have only been heightened by their tendency to avoid such competition where possible. "Black young people, in particular," the authors state, "seem to place a strong negative value on intellectual competition" (1985, p. 17). The public's tendency to impute intellectual inferiority to genetic (ability) factors has only intensified blacks' fears and doubts about themselves.

This self-defeating ethos is the outcome of an effective societal expectancy that diminishes many blacks' intensity of effort, level of concentration, and willingness to take risks—key factors in the development of self-confidence and new skills—and perversely makes them explain their failures in terms of their ability rather than their effort. Thus, say the authors, "each engagement in intellectual competition carries the weight of a test of one's own genetic endowment and that of black people as a whole" (1985, p. 19). No wonder many recoil from any situation where the rumor of inferiority may be proved true.

These mental barriers to competition and performance are just as real as the Jim Crow laws, which obstructed blacks' mobility and civic participation. They can be overcome, the authors suggest, by deliberate control of how blacks talk to one another in terms of their mutual expectations, by creation in black communities of an "intellectual work ethic," and by teaching young blacks to attribute intellectual success to their effort and not to their innate ability.

Certainly not everyone under the yolk of economic deprivation succumbs to fatalism. There are many have-not adults and young people who retain an intact internal locus of control, a sense that they control their lives through effort and application. Neighborhood organizing for urban school reform is built around these people. How do parents and children interact so as to preserve this sense of efficacy?

PARENT-CHILD INTERACTION STYLES AND SCHOOL SUCCESS

Reginald Clark (1983) studied the different styles of interaction between adults and children in low-income families in Chicago. His work went beyond Ogbu's in examining the types of interactions within families that lead to success or failure in the child's academic work. He studied ten families intensively, five of which had an adolescent in secondary school who was achieving academically and five in which the adolescent was failing badly. In the high-achieving group, two families had both parents in the home, the other three had only one. A similar differentiation held for the low-achieving group.

Families of the high achievers engaged in several processes that were noticeably absent in the low-achieving families:

1. These parents explicitly nurtured literacy by encouraging the child to read and write about topical issues and to talk to them about them.
2. They explicitly practiced social etiquette, engaged in word games, and encouraged hobbies.
3. Their style of communication was interactive: they gave direct instruction, but they also gave opportunities for feedback and reinforcements when appropriate.
4. The emotional climate of the household was supportive and discipline was firm but not harsh.

Overall, these parents, though poor by any economic standard, expressed greater optimism and internal locus of control than did their counterparts on the low-achieving end of the scale. Although the single parents lacked some of the parental interactions of the two-parent families, they seemed to persevere by sheer willpower and determination.

In general, the parents of high achievers "sponsored their independence." In other words, they defined the limits of appropriate behavior, then allocated money and other resources, to the extent they could, and delegated responsibility to these adolescents. The high-achieving students thereby gained multiple opportunities to play leadership roles in home academic tasks, leisure tasks, or household maintenance tasks. Parents set schedules and routines, monitored their offsprings' friends and other social contacts, and taught them self-protection.

The family life of low achievers was much harder for Clark to analyze because of the greater difficulty in obtaining data. These people he characterized as hurt, embarrassed, scarred, and uncommunicative. The father in those families, where there was a father, had not really been involved in childrearing; the mother in every case had developed a sense of helplessness and frustration with life and was still working through her own childhood traumas. Clark, a compassionate observer of these ongoing tragedies, commented with sad anger that "these cases demonstrate the degree of home abuse one can withstand at various stages in the lifecycle and still be considered legally sane" (1983, p. 171).

Clark's cases represented two extremes: those whose lives were out of control under the degrading conditions of poverty and those who maintained control. The low-to-moderate income population should not be thought of in these either-or terms. Most people in such circumstances fall somewhere in between states of complete helplessness or being psychologically on top of things in spite of it all.

IMPLICATIONS OF REASSESSING VICTIMHOOD

There is a structural relationship between haves and have-nots whereby the have-nots are, for the most part, kept in their disadvantaged position. It is not as obvious as the officially sanctioned apartheid of South Africa, but it is the result of the functioning of the economic and political institutions of American society, which makes wealth and power flow from the poor to the well-off. This structure is held in place by a diversity of behaviors and internalized attitudes and theories that in one way or another either blame the victim or ignore the relationship between victim and victimizer groups. Have-nots themselves often fall prey to self-defeating attitudes that lead to lowered intellectual performance, as in the case of students; inappropriate behaviors with regard to school personnel on the part of parents; or for both, a generalized anxiety with regard to competition in American society.

The studies mentioned in this chapter have focused on blacks. Many of the authors of the studies are black. Other minorities, especially Latinos and Native Americans, have been studied much less, until recently, because few of their number have been in a position to do so. But the adaptive mechanisms described are applicable whatever the race or ethnicity of the oppressed. It is also important to keep in mind that although self-defeating attitudes are system-produced, they are not inevitable. Many have-nots are not fatalistic, but still they encounter systematic obstruction and discrimination. Tenacity alone keeps them going.

The prescription by some, for example, Howard and Hammond (1985), that organizing should take the form of exhortation within the have-not community to develop self-reliance and self-confidence, has found form in the Reverend Jesse Jackson's EXCEL program.[3] While the development of racial pride is a laudable and even essential goal, it is not achieved merely through quasi-religious group exercises. Organization for collective action must acknowledge, first, that systems and institutions oppress, and then, understand how they do so, formulate strategies based on these realities, and act upon them. Only within this context will exhortatory speeches and educational campaigns carry over into changed practices. Having reassessed the conditions of have-nots, our investigation now turns its full attention to the inner-city school.

3

The Failures of
Inner-City Public Schools

The poor do not learn because they are not taught.
(Payne, 1984, p. 143)

The symptoms of the problem are too painfully well known. Truancy rates in many inner-city schools range between 40 and 70 percent. Dropout rates in high school approach 50 percent among Hispanics, especially Mexican-Americans and Puerto Ricans; rates for low-income blacks are nearly as high. Those minority youngsters who do finish high school consistently score lower than whites on SAT exams. Only 7 percent of Hispanics and 12 percent of blacks finish college compared with 23 percent of whites (Levin, 1987).

Arguably, there are some good schools in poor urban neighborhoods. There is a significant black middle-class population. There are large numbers of foreign-born students, black, Hispanic, Asian, in every urban system who do well academically. Desegregation orders have dispersed tens of thousands of low-income minority students nationally into schools in more affluent areas. Yet these facts only serve to intensify the overall picture of urban school failure. In general, if an urban student is from low-income circumstances and is not white, that student is at a considerably heightened risk of failure in school.

This chapter probes the weaknesses in schools and school systems that are responsible for this catastrophic social evil, beginning with the teacher in the classroom and moving to the urban system as a whole. A brief look at current popular calls for reform explains why the reform agenda is unfinished.

THE INNER-CITY CLASSROOM

When have-not parents criticize schools, they usually do so in terms of teacher abuse and neglect of their children; either teachers are racially prejudiced toward them or they do not demand enough of them academically. In educators' jargon, these are the issues of culture shock and teacher expectations. Overcoming problems in these areas of attitude will go far to improve student motivation and discipline, but curriculum must also be drastically enhanced. Individual classrooms, of course, cannot be improved without positive change in the entire school and indeed the whole system itself. We merely begin the analysis with the classroom.

Culture Shock

Teacher culture shock is a combination of ignorance of the life ways of the poor and a reaction based on a position of power with respect to the poor. Gerry Rosenfeld (1971) spent six years as a teacher and participant observer in a Harlem grade school; his anthropological study revealed that the teachers insisted on classroom practice that ran against the slum child's experiences. They did so out of ignorance of the child's home and neighborhood environment. Although the inner-city child may have had limited experience outside his physical neighborhood, he had extensive social contact with a wide diversity of other people on its streets and in its shops. Home was a crowded place as well. The suburban child usually encounters the opposite: wide physical distance but much less social interaction. To Rosenfeld, "the school appeared sometimes as the place where activity came to a halt" (1971, p. 31). The result was that a great deal of the teacher's time was taken up with making the children sit still. Subject matter under such constraints became fragmented, unrelated to the child's life beyond the school, and disconnected within itself. Thus children found school not only incredibly dull but punishing as well. Accordingly they developed a number of physical and psychological defenses, from overt hostility or withdrawal to gamesmanship.

Teachers, frustrated and discontented with their inability to teach (rooted in their lack of understanding of the child's experience), had over the years developed "an arsenal of techniques and maneuvers . . . by which to subjugate and pacify children" (Rosenfeld, 1971, p. 45). Such abuse was often verbal. For example, some teachers would denigrate the child's appearance: "Shut those thick lips!" or "prehensile lips!" or make unconsciously prejudiced remarks complaining about the children's off-key singing of the national anthem "when we know that all blacks are musical." Other, more vicious abuse included one teacher's practice of locking a child in a metal closet for speaking without raising his hand. The teacher would then pound on its sides, making a deafening noise. Other teachers delighted in threatening to summon parents of children they knew were orphans or who had no parent living at home. One teacher regularly burned or consigned to the trash the children's homework, even as they watched. Hitting, slapping, poking, ear-tweaking, and hair-pulling were almost universal forms of informal punishment.

Rosenfeld's book was one of a type coming out of the late 1960s that characterized inner-city schools, especially elementary schools, as jails or concentration camps where teachers acted as sadistic guards, heaping violent punishment and verbal abuse on students. These things did happen, and they probably still do happen, though less often because of a changed climate with regard to litigation and student rights. The root of most abuse is the overreaction by teachers to the differences between their own middle-class values and behaviors and the street-corner behavior of their charges. The greater abuse, however, derives from their lowered expectancies of these children, a subject we will explore shortly.

How, Rosenfeld asked, could a school continue to survive and perpetuate itself even though it does not serve to support its individual members? He concluded that, over time, humans will unconsciously adapt their behavior to the system's demands rather than oppose it. As people's behavior changes to adapt to a system—in this case the new teachers became more punishing and abusive over the years—they rationalize these changes, a process that Payne called the rationalization of inequality or the justification of injustice (Payne, 1984). Teachers at the Harlem school denied abusing the children, claiming that the children's misbehavior brought punishment upon themselves. Unfortunately, the teachers may have met their need to vent their frustrations, but they were still unhappy in their jobs.

Inner-city teachers often make one of two errors in assessing how their students are different from themselves. The first and much more common error sees inner-city schools as holding pens filled with psychotics, junkies, hustlers, and lesser ne'er-do-wells (Betts, 1978). This view overgeneralizes to the detriment of the vast majority of students who can profit from good instruction. The second error minimizes differences lest the students be stereotyped. This latter view may be held by middle-class white teachers in predominantly minority schools who are committed to the service of these children. Let me give an example of this second view.

Some years ago I was consulting with a group of elementary faculty, most of whom were white, in a school whose population was virtually all black working-class youth. One of the white teachers, who had been identified privately by the black principal as one of his better teachers, asked me to conduct a session on "understanding the urban child." Further probing revealed that she meant the black children she taught. She had been with these children almost daily for five years, yet she was only now coming to the realization that she did not understand the subculture from which they came.

Refusal to acknowledge cultural differences can be as detrimental to effective instruction as seeing the students as the crazed enemy. Herbert Foster (1974), a teacher for twenty years in New York City's special education high schools, has compiled an accurate and comprehensive description of black street-corner language, dress, and general behavior. Any inner-city teacher reading this work will immediately recognize the precision of Foster's assertions, although dress and language will vary over time and distance; for example, New York in 1975 is not Milwaukee in 1985. There is a unique emphasis on verbal skills in a black street-corner society that middle-class people are unaccustomed to. Foster describes gamesmanship, taunting, and other forms of verbal jousting as "woofing," "ribbin'," "jivin'," and "playin' the dozens." Since language conveys the culture, he spends the greater part of his book examining language forms and the beliefs they contain, based both on his extensive experience and the literature in the field.[1] He also painstakingly analyzes dress styles.

Challenging or testing teachers, done by all students in all schools, takes on new meanings when it is done in inner-city schools by poor minority youth. Because it is done in an unfamiliar mode, the teacher is more likely to react out of fear or anger. By the same token, street-corner students, conditioned to act in certain physical, aggressive, and sexual ways and used to strong physical control, also become disoriented and do not understand the teacher's behavior.[2] The result too often is an escalation of acting out, disruption, and disorder.

On the secondary level, Foster continues, because children are now bigger and more able to retaliate, any teacher who attempts to replicate the punishing behavior meted out years earlier does so at great risk to life and limb. Yet overreaction based on lack of understanding is still the order of the day.

Foster suggests that teachers can develop through four stages in their relationships with students as they gain experience in teaching. The first two stages are closely linked and grounded in the cultural disparity between middle-class teacher and street-corner students. The new teacher, initially idealistic, wishes to be "friends" with the students, but street-corner students, expecting the teacher to make them behave, begin their testing games immediately. According to Foster, the teacher often becomes "fearful, humiliated, frustrated, and isolated, even though only a few of his students are testing him" (1974, p. 245). The result is chaos, because children accustomed to being handled by threats and punishment are likely to interpret friendliness as a sign of weakness. At the outset, a teacher should adopt a business-like manner that avoids either excessive friendliness or harshness.

In Foster's third stage, discipline, the teacher asserts himself and takes control of the class. But it can be a rigid, untrusting control. Foster estimates that up to 80 percent of the teachers who stay in inner-city teaching remain fixated at this level, never expressing positive feelings. A few teachers reach his fourth stage, humanization, in which students are secure and there is mutual respect among all in the class. Teachers who reach this ultimate stage, Foster claims, possess inner strength, good humor, and warmth. They are organized in their work, physically energetic, and self-accepting, and they not only do not fear their students, but they know that the students can learn.

Foster's approach to change focuses exclusively on the individual teacher; he does not address certain structural problems at all. For example, the departmental organization of the high school, wherein students change classes five or six times daily, coupled with high truancy rates, guarantees that the teacher will encounter most students on a sporadic basis, making it very difficult to establish stable relation-ships with students at all. In addition, teacher transiency into and out of inner-city schools is common. An inner-city student is much more likely than his outer-city counterpart to experience long-term substi-tute teachers, new and inexperienced teachers, or experienced teachers with unsatisfactory ratings who are shuttled from school to school in what one superintendent called "the annual dance of the lemons." These structurally unstabilizing forces underlie and exacer-bate the problem of culture shock.

Culture shock in inner-city schools is more commonly manifested by creating an atmosphere of lowered expectations of students by school personnel than by their overreacting in harsh and punitive ways to the cultural differences street-corner youngsters bring to school with them. When Payne began his study of Westside High in Chicago, he expected to encounter teachers actively putting down black stu-dents' attempts to learn. What he found instead was an almost univer-sal apathy toward achievement on the part of both staff and students. He noted angrily that if he could have inscribed in stone over the entrance the motto that best described the school, it would be the phrase "It ain't my job!" (Payne, 1984, p. 58). Teachers took little responsibility for students' learning, and students accommodated this laissez-faire attitude. Although in this case, expectations for performance from the top of the system on down were low, this study made clear that teacher expectations, flowing from the culture shock just discussed, can be a powerful negative influence on student learning. The next section analyzes how they operate in the classroom.

Teacher Expectations and Student Achievement

In 1968, Robert Rosenthal and Lenore Jacobson published their now famous investigation into the relationship between teacher expectations and student achievement, entitled *Pygmalion in the Classroom*. Their work was to become the subject of considerable controversy and the catalyst for at least several hundred more studies of the hypothesis that teachers' low expectations are the primary reason for their pupils' failure in school. As a result we have a much clearer picture of how the process works, but we should be cautious in attributing too much to this element alone. Teacher expectations may be an important element in student failure, but they are not independent of the entire context of organizational maladaptation.

The original model of teacher expectation effects had four basic aspects (Cooper & Good, 1983):

1. The teacher develops expectations about the behavior and achievement of each student.
2. The teacher behaves differently with each student according to these expectations.
3. This teacher behavior informs the student about the behavior and achievement the teacher expects and is thought to affect the student's self-concept, level of motivation, and level of aspiration.
4. If the teacher is consistent in these behaviors over time and if the student complies, the student's achievement will conform with the teacher's belief.

There is a strong link between a teacher's expectations of his students and his behavior toward them. Teachers will act more warmly toward students of whom they have higher expectations (HE students). They are more likely to praise them, challenge them, and encourage them to persist.

The teacher's sense of how well he controls the classroom also affects his behavior toward students. When he has low expectations of certain students (LE students), the well-meaning teacher usually tries to inhibit their disruptive behavior by ignoring or criticizing them publicly, then compensating for this punishment by seeking the students out privately and talking positively with them. Research suggests that if the teacher wishes to communicate positively with LE students, this public punishment must be minimized, and there must be appropriate private positive feedback. In addition, the teacher must counter his tendency to ignore quiet LE students by increasing these students' participation with positive reinforcements (paying close attention, head-nodding, or expressions of agreement when they do participate).

It is possible for a teacher to control classroom behavior yet still have many students fail. When this scenario occurs, the students combine a poor sense of control over their own academic learning with low self-esteem. Saying to a student, for example, that she *can* write well, when both student and teacher are aware of her deficits, or showing ignorance of street-corner word games, can make the student think to herself, "I'm stuck with this ignorant teacher. I must not be worth having a good teacher." This type of attitude can certainly dampen academic effort, if not lead to uncooperative or disruptive behaviors. Hence, teacher praise, to be appropriate, must be reinforcing, directed to specific behaviors, and be believable.

Conversely, students can have good self-esteem but lack a sense of control over their learning. I recall one student in my ninth-grade inner-city math class who became very angry at me for not establishing control of my class, even though I had only been in the school for a few weeks. All the students were black, most were low-income, and the majority exhibited the street-corner behaviors that Foster described. As the new teacher, I was also proceeding as Foster predicted. The chaos was considerable; I could never lecture, so I used worksheets that students could work on at their own pace. Most students would finish one during the class period. Dorothy could finish three or four during the same time, since much of the work was relatively unchallenging for her. Her anger was due to her frustration with the chaotic classroom environment; she felt she was in a holding pattern, and she was. I have no doubt that Dorothy had good self-esteem, but she had little sense of control over her own learning outcomes.

The teacher who establishes control in the classroom has moved to Foster's third stage. Control is a result not only of a feeling of physical security but also of stability in the group over time, of a teacher's knowledge of students' life conditions, and of schoolwide, systemic, and community factors that enhance communication and provide sufficient resources and sense of control among all the actors. Control, however, is not enough by itself. If the communication of teacher expectations is to affect the students' self-esteem and level of motivation, it must emphasize appropriate positive feedback and the message that students are not only responsible for their own learning, but if they put in the effort, they *will* learn. Ultimately the matter of control in the classroom must evolve to a mutual sense of control, shared between the teacher and students, if most students are to achieve at their potential.

Ineffective Instruction: Basic Skills versus Higher-Order Learning

A considerable debate has waxed and waned over whether or not the American public school can be an interesting place, a place where students are motivated to learn (Sarason, 1983; Cusick, 1983). In schools where teachers and students are secure and respect one another, a further ingredient is required for motivation to learn: a curriculum that develops higher-order thinking skills and positive affective outcomes. Visitors to these effective schools will discover motivation and self-discipline aplenty.

Two former teachers, Bertha Davis and Dorothy Arnof (1983), have written a clear, highly prescriptive, and useful book on these curriculum matters, entitled *How to Fix What's Wrong with Our Schools*. Their focus is on what teachers do in classrooms that is ineffective and on what they should do by contrast.

There is ample evidence, they claim, that poor practice in teaching reading begins in fourth grade. Sentences in earlier grade readers were short; the words and ideas were well within the experience of the pupils. Beginning with fourth grade, however, reading changes. Students are expected to do progressively more reading outside their readers from other sources. There are new ideas outside their experience; words they have never spoken are introduced; sentences become longer and more complex. Students must learn to put details under the big ideas, to summarize, to outline, to adapt their reading styles to the material, and to detect logical flaws and biases.

Students must be taught to do these things, but they are not, because reading from the fourth grade on is approached in terms of content assimilation and recall rather than as a process of thinking. Since the mature reader must be an active reasoner, the task of instruction changes drastically; but the instruction does not. Teachers still tend to focus on vocabulary, the meanings of single, isolated words, and to ignore follow-up exercises that would help students work through meanings of sentence groups by looking for clues, such as signal words or punctuation. One exception to lack of follow-up, however, is a project (such as, "make a collage about Martin Luther

King, Jr."), but such projects contribute little to growth in these higher-order reading skills.

Why do teachers behave this way? The authors claim that it is because many teachers themselves are not thinking readers. Another reason is that, since there may be a range of up to five grades in reading ability in a single classroom, teachers not skilled in individualizing classwork may tend to teach to the lower levels and not challenge those students able to do more. A further cause is that many teachers finally succumb to the temptation to gear reading difficulty to the students' independent reading level, that is, the level at which a student will spontaneously read material. Such material is usually not challenging. A final reason is that it is quite easy to avoid the hard work of teaching reading as thinking. Despite these reasons, material should be chosen for its "conceptual freight," not merely its sentence length or number of words on a "familiar words" list.

Problems in mathematics skill development parallel those in reading. Although computation skills appear to be taught well in the first three grades, problem-solving skills, especially those dealing with verbal math problems, are not. After grade three, children are not regularly introduced to such problems. They are not taught to see what the problem is, how to develop strategies for solving it (for example, by asking further questions), to work through these strategies, and finally to step back and see what worked, what did not, and what further questions need to be dealt with. In addition, teachers of students who speak in black English vernacular should familiarize themselves with the ways in which this nonstandard dialect can interfere with understanding of verbal problems in mathematics and science posed in Standard English (Orr, 1987).

The teaching of writing is also badly served, Davis and Arnof claim. Most school staffs have not agreed on what constitutes acceptable writing and what does not at each grade level. Assigning, collecting, and grading writing is not teaching writing. There should be a prewriting period in which ideas are generated through discussion or brainstorming, then a writing period in which the teacher also writes, and finally a postwriting session, during which samples of student writing are anonymously examined in class for success or lack of it in stating purpose, in keeping the audience in mind, or in mechanics. Too much emphasis is placed on mechanics in the early grades and not enough on the communication aspect of writing. Davis and Arnof assert that formal grammar should not be taught before eighth or ninth grade.

Criticism of writing instruction—or the lack of it—in schools leads to discussion of teaching study skills. Davis and Arnof state emphatically, "We have never seen, in any school, a skills program that made sense" (1983, p. 61). Outlining, for instance, is a global skill that can only be taught by teaching its subskills. How often does a teacher write an outline on the board, require the students to copy it, and then claim to have taught how to outline? Necessary subskills would be taught by exercises, for example, that would ask students to differentiate big ideas and little ideas from a list. Research papers, of course, demand many subskills. Exercises in taking notes by reducing sentences or paragraphs to key words or phrases, in selecting material relevant to a topic, or in moving from an encyclopedia article to other sources for more detailed information are essential.

In the inner-city school, these poor instruction patterns are exaggerated. Even the so-called basic skills of the first three grades may not be taught. Teachers confronted with children of low-income families may, with the best of intentions, challenge them even less than their middle-income counterparts, despite evidence that children from deprived circumstances can learn. Another difficulty is that inner-city teachers do not know how to individualize instruction to combat absenteeism, or if they do know, they do not do it because it takes greater energy and is not required or supported by the school's administration. The authors assert correctly that classrooms that hold a higher percentage of children with learning deficiencies need excellent teachers who can break lessons into understandable, interesting bits and build from there, who can use visual means to get messages across, and who can continue the quest for more appropriate instructional approaches through rigorous self-reflection.

The inner-city classroom is an arena where class and race differences sometimes clash violently, though the more typical responses of teacher and student alike are to withdraw from the confrontation into a world of drift and lowered expectations. Nonetheless there are inner-city teachers who love their work, are good at it, and see no need for change in what they do. These are teachers, according to Davis and Arnof, "whose classroom students are *purposefully* and *successfully* engaged in *worthwhile* and *appropriate* learning experiences" (1983, p. 87). Laymen, as well as principals and their own colleagues, know who these teachers are, although Davis and Arnof assert that only a qualified professional—a "senior teacher," a position which unfortunately does not yet exist in most school systems—can supervise a teacher in order to develop that teacher's classroom effectiveness.

These teachers too often do not grow old in teaching. They leave teaching too soon. No teacher operates a classroom in a vacuum. The school's organizational climate, the teacher's peers and supervisors, and the district's modes of support all profoundly influence what a teacher is and is not able to accomplish. The next section discusses the organizational characteristics of schools and school systems.

THE SCHOOL AS SYSTEM

The Persistence of the Machine Model of Schooling

Most of us still think of the urban school system in terms of the machine bureaucracy. This original model, formulated in the management theories of Max Weber and Frederick Taylor from 1900 and 1930, viewed the organization from the top.[3] The individual was a rational actor in a closed system, an obedient functionary in an orderly, stable hierarchy of authority, controlled solely from within. Those at the top of the pyramid handed down orders and made rules. The domains of influence within the system were fixed jurisdictions. The performance roles connected with these domains were standardized so that the actors within them could be thought of as interchangeable parts. In order to ensure clarity and rationality of control, communication was made formal by written directives, memos, reports, evaluations, and formal conferences. Blue ink was the lifeblood of the bureaucracy (Webb, 1981, p. 208). The whole system was characterized by inflexibility, objectivity, and rational control, all to create greater predictability of outcome.

Although these ideas were applied to school system and factory alike around the turn of the century, by 1930 it was apparent that they did not fit reality. Organizational theory now acknowledges that the system actors have inclinations of their own and act idiosyncratically, and that the system itself is not closed but is susceptible in countless ways to its organizational environment.

Thus the urban school system is both machine and organism. So to clamor for more efficiency, in terms of improved supervision, more testing, more precise objectives, and other forms of quality control, is to miss the mark because it fails to consider the paradoxes attendant upon openness to the environment and to human social actors (Callahan, 1962). Education simply cannot "be delivered"; students and parents are social actors at one and the same time inside of and outside of the system (Seeley, 1981).

A chief characteristic of the system-as-organism is that it grows and expands. It does this for several reasons: to accomplish its tasks, to resolve internal stresses and conflicts, to adapt to a changing environ-

ment (Katz & Kahn, 1978). In addition, the roles and norms of bureaucracy are ripe for ever more elaboration; even the ideology of organization itself encourages growth. In recent years the heightened impact
on urban systems by the federal government, courts, citizen and other
pressure groups, the media, and colleges of education, among other
forces, have driven these systems to bewildering states of complexity.
Even smaller school systems show this tendency to expand and grow
in complexity in response to environmental demands. Listen to Ernest
Boyer (1983):

> In one suburban school we visited, a teacher voiced resentment. "In
> 1968," she said, "We had 104 people in our central office and 28,000
> students in the school system. Now we have 140 staff people in the central
> office, plus their secretaries, but only 19,000 students. (p. 225)

Even though student enrollment had dropped 32 percent in 15 years,
administrative staffing had increased over 35 percent during the same
period!

Modern bureaucracies also reveal their actors as individuals capable of idiosyncratic behavior. With regard to schools, several investigators have named this tendency toward internal inconsistency the
"loosely coupled system" (Purkey & Smith, 1983, p. 441). According to
this view, teachers are relatively independent of administrative supervision, much more so than one would expect in the classical machine
bureaucracy. Although this autonomy gives teachers independence
from supervision, it can also magnify their sense of isolation, inse-
curity, and inefficacy. This isolation increases their power inside the
classroom while reducing their power outside it (Joyce, Hersh, &
McKibbin, 1983).

Principals, central office administrators, and board members also
occupy ambiguous niches in the loosely coupled system. Carrying
responsibility for outcomes often without corresponding actual power
to implement them can produce counterproductive, manipulative behavior, usually in the form of withholding information (Borman &
Spring, 1984). Those most likely to take the brunt of this internal
inconsistency are parents and students.

Urban school systems are thus organic in two ways. First, they are
self-maintaining, adaptive, and tend toward growth; hence, they are
extraordinarily sensitive or vulnerable to environmental pressures.
Second, they are loosely coupled, which renders them susceptible to
all the obstructions and willfulness that human actors can generate.
Another factor that complicates the loose-coupling phenomenon is

the set of cultural beliefs and norms held by the system actors. It may be valid to explain school outcomes in terms of individualistic psychology, but such explanations are incomplete. They must take into consideration the social environment within the school and the system.

After considerable study, Seymour Sarason (1971) concluded that teachers' beliefs about certain "basic regularities" of school are not internally derived but are the product of the social environment, that is, supervisors' requirements, peer reinforcements, or student expectations. These regularities are the outward expression of strong, largely unexamined beliefs about education. An example is the requirement that every child from first through twelfth grade must manipulate numbers daily.

These beliefs may hide the seeds of conflict ("We should tell students what to study, but we should also hook their interest"). They may severely limit critical thinking ("Parents are important but ancillary actors in the student's education." "Education is a service to be delivered"). Or they may be self-contradictory ("It is possible for teachers to create conditions for interesting learning experiences when these conditions do not exist for the teachers themselves").

These beliefs are remarkable primarily because they are the unseen reefs upon which attempts at change can founder. They can form obstacles to constructive change precisely because they are not comprehended as anything other than the way things are. They can obstruct the creation of models of reality that will allow things to be different, or they can drastically reshape those models when they are applied. Organizing must expose these beliefs and publicly challenge them where necessary.

School Funding Inequities

One of the principal beliefs relevant to our discussion of the low quality of schools for the poor is that these schools *should* be of low quality. This legacy of race and class prejudice as an overriding belief has produced gross systematic inequities in public schools for as long as they have existed. For the first hundred years after publicly supported education became available to blacks, these schools were planned to be inferior (Weinberg, 1983). Funding was inadequate, teachers were less trained, buildings were insufficient, school terms were shorter, and supplies were scarce or unavailable. In short, school systems institutionalized racism and discrimination, and despite reforms grounded in the 1954 Brown decision and its legal antecedents, many still embody such oppression through the distribution of their financial resources.

Virtually all research on school finance has focused on how districts differ from one another in their per-pupil expenditures. That urban centers have fewer resources than their suburban counterparts has been obvious. But what is less well known is the extent of inequality of resource distribution within a particular district, especially one with a significant percentage of minority and/or low-income pupils. A further area of inequality is the distribution from classroom to classroom within a given urban school.

It should be noted that inadequate financial and personnel resources are standard complaints by minority and low-income parents. Inner-city school buildings are usually older, less well maintained, and less well furnished. Teacher turnover is frequent, and replacement teachers are younger and less experienced than teachers in middle-class white neighborhood schools. Getting hard data on these inequities has historically been very difficult to do. When Chicago and other large cities refused to cooperate in the federally mandated Equal Educational Opportunities Survey (Coleman Report) in 1965, the federal authorities allowed their defiance to stand. Meyer Weinberg (1983) noted that "school systems are virtually free of external checks on the final disposition of enormous tax funds, a prerogative school boards and superintendents guard most jealously" (p. 141).

Few researchers have paid attention to intradistrict inequalities since 1954. Before this time, legally segregated systems such as Washington, D.C., actively fostered inequities. Yet there is evidence of continuing bias against low-income and minority students. A 1961 study of Detroit's public schools, which were then 29 percent black, demonstrated systematic bias in the distribution of school resources to schools attended by low-income children, both black and white (Weinberg, 1983). A 1971 study (Guthrie et al.), primarily focusing on Michigan, discovered systematic school resource distribution bias against minority low-income children on cross-district, within-district, and between-classroom levels. Other studies concluded that teachers in classrooms serving predominantly poor children tended to be younger, less experienced, and therefore less likely to be tenured. The U.S. Office of Civil Rights studied intradistrict inequalities in New York City from 1973 to 1977. It found that schools serving minority children were likely to get up to 15 percent less funding, unequal educational services in terms of personnel, and ineffective counseling—all of which channel such children disproportionately toward vocational and special programs. Even desegregated school systems can continue to discriminate against poor children by means of tracking within a school, by ability grouping within a classroom, or by using teacher transfer policies to the advantage of the white middle class.

The following case study embodies most of the points raised in this section about the inadequacy of the machine model of school organization. It shows how some parents and other citizens organized to exploit a school's organic openness to the environment, loose coupling, and teacher beliefs. Yet it also demonstrates that school systems steeped in discriminatory attitudes are, in turn, highly responsive to neighborhood organizing also rooted in prejudice. At the same time, this study shows the unreliability of the theory that the failure of low-income children is due to the clash of their culture with the middle-class culture of the school. Rather, the conclusion should be that the school is the cause of the failure.

A Case Study of Discrimination in Neighborhood Organizing

R. Timothy Sieber (1982) investigated how upper middle-class white parents engaged in an intense political struggle with the local public school to promote their own children's academic success. Upper middle-class professionals had gentrified parts of New York's fictitiously named Chestnut Heights section, buying and renovating the stately old brownstone homes. Thus they came to be known as the "brownstoners." Three generations of Irish, Italian, and Syrian working-class families were the majority of its population, however. But since these "old-timers" sent many of their children to parochial schools, the Puerto Ricans, inhabiting tenements along the neighborhood's borders, made up a majority of the families in the local elementary school, P.S. 4. The school's staff was traditionalist, many of Jewish working-class backgrounds.

The brownstoners, geographically mobile, affluent, permissive in their childrearing style, were also politically astute and aggressive. They formed the Chestnut Heights Association (CHA), not only to promote historic preservation and cleanup projects but also to fight hospital expansion and expressway construction that would take big bites out of neighborhood housing. They also organized a reform Democratic Party organization that ousted the local old-timer-dominated regular organization.

Although most brownstoners sent their children to private schools in the area, some enrolled at P.S. 4. However, brownstoner parents from both P.S. 4 and private schools saw it as their civic duty to improve the public school. They formed an action committee under the umbrella of CHA and began to press their concerns on the public school. Initially they gained regular access to the school, gathered information on school practices and personnel, and generally established their social presence. They then organized a tutoring program in reading, volunteered in the school library, and engineered a takeover of the PTA, a group previously dominated by teachers but whose parent membership had been exclusively Puerto Rican.

The brownstoners were paternalistic toward staff and traditionalist parents, Puerto Rican and old-timer alike. Eventually they demanded and achieved creation of an open-format setting in the highest track class in each grade; this was to be the only track for brownstoner children, even for those whose parents admitted that their children were slow learners. Not only were brownstoner adults aloof and insulated from the other groups in the neighborhood, their children also segregated themselves from the other neighborhood groups in the school.

In the classroom, brownstoner children were given access to creative arts, from painting and sculpture to crafts, poetry writing, and drama production. Other classes did none of these. They had materials, such as Cuisenaire rods and geoboards, that the other classes did not have. They were given many opportunities to address their class formally in debates, reporting, poetry reading, or explaining artwork and were allowed to talk to their classmates informally and work cooperatively with them throughout the day. The lower classes continued to be teacher-centered and standardized in curriculum matters. Discipline was looser for brownstoner children; their seats were moveable, and they were reprimanded, if at all, only verbally. Lower-class seats were fixed to the floor, and physical punishment by teachers was frequent.

The teachers' attitudes toward brownstoners were ambivalent. Although they took pride in the academic success of these children and in the high socioeconomic status of their doctor-lawyer-writer-architect parents, they felt that these children were spoiled and overprivileged and that they and their parents were condescending to the teachers and pushy at times. Their cosmopolitan life-style irritated teachers who resented the children's informal attire at school, their casual attitude toward their own lateness, and their assumption that normal rules could be overridden in their favor. For their part, brownstoner parents looked down on teachers as socially unsophisticated and provincial in outlook and manners.

Despite the school's accommodation to many of the brownstoner parents' demands, teachers retained their professional autonomy with regard to parents, who continued to meet bureaucratic obstacles in their attempts to gain access to teachers or information about their children or school classes.

This study highlights several important points. First, the brownstoner parents' struggle with the local public school was through the neighborhood association to which they belonged. This connection linked them with others in the neighborhood who did not have children in P.S. 4 but who understood that its improvement was part of overall neighborhood improvement.

Second, the brownstoners understood how sensitive public schools are to their neighborhood environment despite the machine characteristics that the system exhibits. They dealt with the school with the belief that they were a group with a right to influence in the school. They approached school staff as social actors, not cogs, but individuals who could be swayed to their point of view. The brownstoners took shared responsibility for redirecting school policy by means of their physical presence and by their initiation of programs and volunteer work. They did not simply press demands by saying, "You do this and that for us." They not only initiated but monitored and followed through, avoiding the pitfalls of the service-delivery model of education. Their political struggle gained for them most of what they sought.

But, third, their largely successful battle underscored how difficult school reform for have-nots' children will be. Despite the brownstoners' high socioeconomic status and sophistication, they continued to encounter resistance from teachers. Even though they had taken over the PTA, the parents were still on the outside, not yet institutionalized into the policymaking process of the school.

Finally, the brownstoners' success through collective action reveals the class and race orientation of the school process. The high socioeconomic status of this parent group provided the wedge into the ordinary school procedures that had heretofore miseducated the Puerto Rican children and changed these regularities significantly enough to accommodate the brownstoner children. It attracted greater resources and further teacher training for the open format. Here was a school miseducating have-not children and blaming them for their failure, yet it could adapt fairly readily to the have children and not miseducate them, despite real cultural differences between the teachers and the brownstoners. The conclusion that the system embodies the racial and class separateness values of the larger society is thus inescapable.

A NOTE ON EFFECTIVE
SCHOOLS RESEARCH AND REFORM

The preceding analysis of schooling failure with inner-city, especially minority, youth requires that we redefine the meaning of school reform. Although the next chapter investigates the strengths and weaknesses of a variety of reform models, this section closes off this overview chapter with a pointed critique of the mainstream reform movements of our day, which are grounded in effective schools research.

Reform in this discussion denotes changes in authority relationships and in the distribution of power and allocation of resources in the school system as a whole (Rich, 1985). It is therefore systematic rather than merely programmatic. It requires program innovation, but it requires much more as well. The connotations of the term reform, in this sense, are that those disenfranchised by the system gain new power and that public systems add appropriate resources to improve their school programs. It assumes that although the system requires drastic overhauling, it is worth salvaging, in opposition to advocates of private alternatives to public schooling or of the complete dismantling of the system.

The mainstream reform movement to promote excellence in education reached a climax in 1983 with the release of several major studies of American education under the sponsorship of important sectors of that establishment or the federal government (Felt, 1985). If there is a single theme that reverberates through all these reports, it is the call for "more": more math, more science, more reading, more homework, more discipline, more school hours, more time on tasks, more "excellence." For example, *A Nation at Risk* (1983), the most ambitiously comprehensive of the reports, pleads for "strengthened" (that is, more) requirements in language, mathematics, science, computers, and social science. Every other report follows suit in its own way.

The excellence movement, as encapsulated in these reports, is essentially a plea for greater effort, efficiency, and productivity in the schools as they are now constituted. Granted that while some critics go beyond this stance, it is now the conventional wisdom. My own experience bears out this last point.

In 1983, I was appointed to our local board's newly created Study Committee on Educational Excellence. Its purpose was to investigate the quality of our public school system. (The Grand Rapids, Michigan, system served about 28,000 K-12 students that year.) Our 19-member committee was both demographically and attitudinally representative of the city. For six months, we met frequently to hear administrator, board, and teacher representatives speak. We held public hearings, visited schools, read whatever we could, and wrangled over the wording of drafts of our report. In the end our report concluded in its preamble that more should be expected of everyone concerned with the schools, from more homework for students to more evaluation of teachers and principals and more money from taxpayers when the system went to them with a millage increase request. The black caucus of our group submitted a minority report stressing the need for special attention to the plight of minority students.

Everyone in our group took the task very seriously. There was near-consensus about what schools were for and how they should accomplish their mission. The labor leader, the high-school student, the college professor, the housewife, the attorney, the warehouseman, the civil rights activist, and the retired telephone company manager all came close to unanimity when discussion of problems and solutions in our public school system led back to the first principles of education. Schools in the United States, they thought, should transmit the rudiments of American culture: its language, its history, and its democratic beliefs. They judged that schools have not achieved this goal as they should. Agreement rested on the least common denominators of minimalist goals and minimum change requirements in the system.

This superficial agreement would have been shattered if reform had come to mean for the group a restructuring of power relationships to include parents, students, and other citizens. Most of the members of this group selected by the school board saw the school system through the educators' eyes, as most reform literature does. The quest for more did not include more power for those "clients" of schools currently disenfranchised. (Even teachers in the worst schools are disenfranchised.)

Effective Schools Research as a Spur to Reform

Buried in Ernest Boyer's 1983 call for reform of America's high schools is the following statement:

> Serving disadvantaged students is the urgent unfinished agenda for American education. Unless we find ways to overcome the problem of failure in the schools, generations of students will continue to be doomed to frustrating, unproductive lives. This nation cannot afford to pay the price of wasted youth. (pp. 246–47)

Boyer's agenda is unfinished because it is largely ignored. Excellence as the current buzzword in many quarters means that schools and school systems should improve themselves by the bootstrap method: without federal help, without local tax increases, and without significant parent or community input. Schools will become effective by somehow imitating the characteristics of those model schools discovered by "effective schools research" (Purkey & Smith, 1983). Yet the schools of the poor, even more in need of aid, are thus at greater risk from bootstrap approaches to reform.

Effective schools research is a small body of literature about the characteristics of schools, predominantly inner-city elementary schools, with a reputation for being "good." These schools were not plagued by disciplinary disruption or low-achievement problems; they also appeared to be socializing children well.

In general, the characteristics of effective schools fall into two categories (Joyce, Hersh, & McKibbin, 1983). The first are tangible aspects of school organization that seem to foster learning, such as staff stability, site autonomy with district support, coherent curriculum, maximized learning time, and opportunities for student responsibility. When they are present, the second category, having to do with less tangible but all-important positive social climate variables, such as a sense of community within the school, teachers' caring for students, and order with discipline, comes into being.

The literature on effectiveness has spawned attempts at reform in several big-city systems, such as Detroit, Chicago, Milwaukee, Memphis, New York, and St. Louis, and in several state departments of education, particularly California, Connecticut, Florida, New Jersey, and Ohio (Ornstein & Levine, 1985). Its appeal for educators is rooted in its focus on the whole school as the setting for reform rather than on individual classrooms; in its apparent precision in identifying tangible variables to be manipulated; and its underlying assumption that reform can occur through increasing efficiency without significantly increased cost. It also lends specificity to the thrust of the more generic excellence reform literature.

Four criticisms of this current reform movement stand out:

1. Disagreements on what constitutes an effective school are really arguments over school purpose.
2. There is overemphasis on testing without a corresponding emphasis on remediation or enrichment when testing exposes deficiencies.

3. The reform literature gives little insight into how to bring about the proposed changes.
4. Virtually no reform literature sees a role for parents and other community members in formulation of schoolwide policy on budget, personnel, and curriculum matters.

Disagreement over school purposes occurs between the minimalist goal of enabling low-income students to perform as well on tests of basic skills as do middle-class students and the more comprehensive goals that would include, for example, development of critical thinking ability, personal growth, and community involvement. Critics of the cult of testing, such as Herb Kohl (1984), Jerrold Coombs (1985), and Kathryn Borman and Joel Spring (1984), contend that the principal dangers of minimum competency testing include labeling of children, distortion of a balanced curriculum (basic skills balanced with critical thinking), reinforcement of the social class sorting process of schools, exacerbation of the dropout rate, and promotion of tendencies to ignore individual differences and the goals of ethical and aesthetic development in students. By itself, a massive program of testing in an urban school system will do no more than pinpoint more accurately its student failures, exposing them to the hostility of a system that is frustrated by them and which frustrates them in return. Unless testing is seen essentially as diagnostic and is connected with effective remediation and enrichment programs (not merely a more narrowly standardized curriculum), it will only aggravate the deterioration of urban schooling. Neighborhood organizers and leaders may attack overemphasis on testing, but they should not attack the tests themselves as culturally biased unless this bias can be easily shown. Rather, low test scores should be used as evidence that the school and the system are not working properly and demands should be made for program changes and inclusion of all actors in the policymaking process.

Current reform trends not only overemphasize test scores, but also provide little insight into how to bring about change (Cuban, 1984). This shortcoming is a methodological one in the case of effective schools research, which is correlational rather than experimental. That is, the investigators identified characteristics (correlates) of good schools but did not manipulate any of them (experiment) to determine effects on school outcomes.

Finally, hardly any of this material allows or encourages a significant role for parents and other community members in the formation of schoolwide policy on budget, personnel, and curriculum matters. Have-not parents and other citizens have organized for educational reform, as this book shows. Schools *can* educate have-not children. Effective schools research has found such programs in the public elementary and secondary sector. There are at least four other success stories in educating the urban poor: Project Head Start, U.S. Armed Forces training programs, parochial schools, and the City University of New York (Berube, 1984).

The few effective educational programs for have-not children give some insight into what should be done as well as hope that it can be done. But it will not be done unless have-not parents organize to demand it. They and their allies in the establishment need insight into how these schools operate dysfunctionally—which this chapter has tried to provide. Yet even inner-city schools can respond positively to public pressure, and have-nots have organized successfully to demand redress for their common grievances. The next chapter examines some current popular models of school reform as a prelude to extensive discussion of the model of neighborhood organizing for urban school reform.

4

The Limits of Popular
Reform Models

Only ordinary citizens can rescue the schools from their sti-
fling corruption, for nobody else wants ordinary children to
become questioning citizens at all. (Karp, 1985, p. 73)

The symptoms of urban school breakdown are widely known. The causes of these problems, however, are subject to considerable debate, as we have seen. The emphasis of this book is on solutions, yet where there is dispute over the sources of the problems, there will be controversy over the solutions.

This chapter explores several approaches to reform, more loosely defined, that have fired the imaginations of those interested in improving urban schools. Although the list is not exhaustive, these approaches provide insight into reform as well as into some blind spots. The ultimate deficiency in each of these conceptualizations of reform is that they either ignore citizen involvement or fail to see it in political terms.

The first four models of reform to be presented command some degree of allegiance in the educational world; the fifth is a hypothetical one suggested by Bruce Joyce, Richard Hersh, and Michael McKibbin (1983), which forms a basis for the model presented in this work. The first model of reform, the packaged innovation, is probably the most widely understood because it grew out of the relationship between educational research institutions and the schools and has been around for decades. Despite evidence that most innovations of the past twenty years have taken root and endured in at least vestigial form, this reform-from-within mode of changing schools has done little to alter them structurally (Owen, Froman, & Moscow, 1981). Rather, the school subculture has tended to absorb the innovation and adapt it to its own ends.

The second model, based on "excellent corporation" research that identifies various attributes found in well-run corporations, disguises the fact that schools, strictly speaking, do not offer a service. While there is a service dimension in that teachers structure and monitor students' learning experiences, the students are not passive consumers, nor are their parents. The third model, the partnership model, does recognize this fact about what schools are to do but avoids the truth of the political nature of the relation between school and community. The last model proposed is that of the influential third party initiating changes. The case study offered does not give much insight into how the community can organize itself for such changes and again avoids school-community political considerations.

Hyperbolic as the quotation opening the chapter may seem— since many in the system profess sincerely that they seek school improvement—it points to the heart of the matter. If urban school reform is to occur, those most oppressed by these schools must "lead the charge." The following section, however, begins the analyses of this chapter by summarizing a study of how school subcultures, those powerful belief systems examined in the preceding chapter, alter innovations incorporated into them. The study illustrates the limits of a model of approaching reform from within the establishment.

THE LIMITS OF PACKAGED INNOVATIONS: THE CASE OF IGE

Individually Guided Education (IGE) was conceived in the mid-1960s by Herbert J. Klausmeier (Popkewitz, Tabachnick, & Wehlage, 1982), a University of Wisconsin professor of educational psychology, as a comprehensive model of school organization and curriculum reform. He and his associates saw several factors in schools that inhibited individualization of instruction. These factors included grouping of children by age; uniformity in programs, textbooks, and materials; norm-referenced (standardized) testing; treatment of teachers without provision for their individual differences; isolation of teachers from colleagues in other schools; and the lack of adaptability of school buildings to independent study. Klausmeier and his associates designed IGE as a system-wide approach to planning and implementing an individualized instructional program for each student.

The IGE model consisted of seven components.

1. The unit, which is a nongraded grouping of 100 students, four teachers, a unit leader, aides, and clerical helpers. Most schools would have several units.

2. The Instructional Programming Model (IPM), a sequence of seven steps staff should follow to "provide efficient ordering, implementation, and evaluation of group and schoolwide objectives" (Popkewitz et al., 1982, p. 29). These seven steps include
   • the statement of educational objectives to be attained by the students;
   • pretest assessment of levels of achievement using criterion-referenced tests (these are tests that indicate whether or not a student can perform a certain task);
   • setting objectives for each child;
   • designing particularized instruction for each child;
   • assessing the success of this instruction;
   • recycling, or
   • reassessing as is appropriate in each case.
3. Evaluation, a formalization implied in IPM.
4. Compatible curriculum materials, including appropriate assessment and record-keeping procedures, as well as a range of printed and other audiovisual materials.
5. Developing home-school-community relations, which involves parents and other citizens in resolving school-related problems.
6. Facilitative environments aiming to coordinate a network of agencies outside the school. These agencies, such as school district policy committees, state associations of IGE schools, teacher education institutions, and other state education institutions, could all reinforce or otherwise assist in the implementation of IGE in the school.
7. Continuing research and development to improve the theory and practice of IGE.

Six schools were chosen for study from among a pool of over 100 that had implemented IGE to some extent. The study sought to answer the following questions: Was the IGE model actually implemented? How was the IGE model changed as it was implemented? Conversely, did the model function as a change agent? That is, did it change the schoolwork patterns of students and the professional ideology of educators?

Institutional Configurations

The research results suggested three different institutional configurations, or ways that the IGE model was put into practice: the technical, the constructive, and the illusory.

The Technical. This configuration, so dubbed by Popkewitz and his associates (1982), seemed closest to the intent of the designers. It was represented by three schools whose student bodies were of considerable diversity (one blue-collar white, one rural poor and racially mixed, one suburban affluent white), yet all three schools displayed remarkably similar characteristics in the way the IGE model was implemented. The teachers and principals saw the schools as managing learning. Knowledge was objective to them. It was measurable, able to be standardized, and taught in discrete steps. The student was seen as deficient in this knowledge, so the process of individualizing instruction entailed assessing each student's deficits and designing an appropriately paced program of largely self-instructional materials and activities. The behaviorist flavor of this teaching-learning interaction was grounded in a search for efficiency and rational planning. The affective domain was officially ignored; teachers gave only peripheral status to creativity, ambiguity, and nonstandardized learning. Overall, the technical configuration seemed to be the logical offspring of the earlier factory-model school of Horace Mann and later psychological theories leading to the development of programmed learning (Callahan, 1962). The parents in each school, however, were in large part supportive of this approach to IGE.

The Constructive. If the first institutional configuration was individualized, the second, called the constructive, was personalized. The name was derived from the students' construction of their own meanings. Only one school fell into this institutional configuration. Knowledge in this school, whose student body was largely from white suburban professional parents, was construed as the personal property of the student. "Work that included plays, music, and art, as well as group activities in social studies and reading, provided opportunities for children to take personal responsibility, initiative, and control in the instructional setting" (1982, p. 116). Teachers had considerable autonomy in designing their instructional objectives. Their interaction with students was give-and-take: students helped decide on the classroom rules and occasionally gave their instructors open criticism, a feedback process the teachers appeared to value highly. Attitudes of "learning should be fun" and "this is the kids' place" introduced elements of spontaneity and creativity that countered the drudgery of classroom routine. The affective domain enjoyed high status here. Emphasis on student interpersonal skills, especially cooperation, and integrated (interdisciplinary) learning tasks underlay the drive to enhance each child's self-image. In sum, educators implemented the IGE model here, but they did so in ways that offset its orientation toward the efficient, the cognitive, the standardized.

Developing the "whole child" in this school had drawbacks, however. Although parents supported the concept, there was conflict with district officials over the standardization of objectives. The researchers also fretted that attention to personal growth seemed to leave the child little privacy; the risk of overemphasis on group means of social control seemed high.

The Illusory. This institutional type characterized two schools whose staffs thought they were using IGE, but by all measures were not. Both schools served poor populations, one black in a large city, the other white in a much smaller city. Teachers thought of their work as "missionaries" to a backward community; they saw students' family and community background as almost hopelessly deficient in the requirements for school learning. Children ran the streets, they said, and there were no reading materials in the home and no appropriate career role models in these low-income families. Where the IGE program would assess a student's lack of knowledge of particular discrete content and devise instruction to remedy this deficit, the illusory schools made little attempt either to diagnose knowledge deficits accurately or to connect instructional activities to them. One startling example given concerned a young girl in a reading carrel with headphones. The printed material she saw was completely different from what she was hearing on the tape machine. The authors made it plain that this was by no means an isolated incident.

Teachers in these schools gave highest priority to obedience; instruction was secondary. When there were discipline or achievement problems—and there were many—teachers led students to believe that the problems originated in themselves. Self-discipline, to these educators, meant acquiescence to control by others. Teachers enforced obedience either by outright physical coercion or more subtle persuasion, which only perpetuated the failure of those they had already condemned as irredeemable.

The types of institutional configuration are summarized in Table 4.1. As these distinct institutional configurations illustrate, the practice of the theoretical model can be drastically altered by the belief systems and conventions, that is, the "culture," of those responsible for its implementation. The literature on school culture demonstrates that schools modify the content of culture and bias it. The process of innovation in these cases demonstrated several ways that this change occurs.

Continued on page 58

TABLE 4.1

IMPLEMENTATION MODES OF IGE MODEL IN SIX PUBLIC SCHOOLS

TYPE OF INSTITUTIONAL CONFIGURATION	TECHNICAL	CONSTRUCTIVE	ILLUSORY
NUMBER OF SCHOOLS STUDIED	3	1	2
DESCRIPTION OF (SCHOOL'S) COMMUNITY	1 Blue-Collar White 1 Rural Poor (Mixed Race) 1 Suburban Affluent White	1 Suburban Professional White	1 Big-City Black Poor 1 Small-City White Poor
PROFESSIONAL IDEOLOGY	Management: School-as-Manager-of-learning Search for efficiency and rational planning as means of control	Teacher autonomy in instructional objectives Negotiated norms (with students) as means of control	School-as-missionary to backward community Preoccupation with traditional means of control, including physical punishment
MEANING OF "INDIVIDUALIZATION"	Pace of instruction varies Behaviorist psychology of learning: programmed instruction	Personalized education: student participates in creating own learning objectives	Purely rhetorical; individualization model not implemented
MEANING OF "KNOWLEDGE"	Knowledge is objective: outside student's mind It is measurable and if standardized, can be taught in discrete steps Basic skills are what all can agree on and test for	Students construct their own meanings They are assumed to have some basic skills from home, other skills are taught Synthetic skills are key	Content = knowledge but content is secondary to obedience as goal of instruction Content not related to instructional method
MEANING OF "STUDENT NEED"	Student is deficient in knowledge, therefore, Diagnose deficiency and specifically instruct to overcome it	Student must become self-determining: instruction must develop the "whole child"	Student's family and community background is deficient; it is questionable whether instruction can overcome this deficit

EMPHASIS ON "AFFECTIVE DOMAIN"	Peripheral status for creativity, ambiguity, and non-standardized learning	Development of student positive self-image through interpersonal skills Learning should be enjoyable: "This is the kids' place."	Ignored formally Informally, student is led to believe problems originate in self
WHAT CONSTITUTES "STUDENT WORK"?	Meet cognitive learning objectives Do worksheets Look industrious	Participate in cooperative problem solving, aesthetic projects (e.g., drama), integrated cognitive tasks; seek self-discovery and interpersonal skills Student has some power to set own objectives and criticize teacher	Be quiet, do own work, do as told, look busy
DIFFICULTIES WITH IMPLEMENTATION AS RESEARCHERS SAW THEM	Ignored affective domain School over routinized Teachers' assumption of consensus on instruction obscured reality of conflict in change?	Attention to whole life of student could leave little privacy Overemphasis on group means of social control Teacher burnout partially due to conflict with district requirements	Reinforced low student self-image and achievement Attempted to indoctrinate both students and parents that self-discipline means control by others

Source: Author's summary of themes from Popkewitz, T., Tabachnick, R., and Wehlage, G. (1982). The myth of educational reform: A study of school responses to a program of change. Madison, WI: University of Wisconsin Press.

Since a basic American value is that efficiency and rationality should characterize our institutions, IGE provided such a vehicle. Much popular criticism of modern schools centers on their inefficiency and unmanageability. Any reform that promises to rectify these conditions has a ready audience.

In addition, reform for teachers, if it does not appear threatening to their job security and working conditions, breaks the monotony of their days and can boost their morale. Participation in reform programs can even enhance their professional self-image. But teachers' conscious openness to reform obscures the fact that as the program takes root in the school building, the educators will develop their own definitions of its abstract terms, such as "individualization" or "students' needs"; they will establish their own priorities and will impose their own beliefs on the model. As a result, the plan of change, in this case IGE, is more susceptible to change itself than are the actual situations in which it is developed. The researchers concluded, in fact, that in none of the six schools were the existing conditions of schooling, in the sense of Sarason's (1971) modal regularities, changed. Institutional reform, from this perspective, though many fervently believe in it, is largely a myth. Institutions demonstrate a remarkable capacity for absorption of reform plans and ritualized adaptation to them, while maintaining their former patterns of behavior. In other words, reform instituted from within the system probably will not change the modal regularities of that system.

Even if the insertion of a prepackaged innovation into a school system is likely to fizzle, could not a holistic model of an excellent large business organization be applied to a school system? They share many aspects, and such an effort may reveal points where the school system could improve its operation. The well-known study by Thomas Peters and Robert Waterman (1982) of excellent large corporations has been discovered by educators and laymen alike as an answer to school reform questions. Comparison does give some good insights, but it suffers from severe limitations at the same time.

THE LIMITS OF EXCELLENT CORPORATION MODELS

Peters and Waterman (1982) sum up their research on excellent large business corporations by listing eight attributes that are usually present in varying degrees:

1. There is a bias for action, as opposed to the "paralysis of analysis" spawned by lengthy market and feasibility studies. These companies experiment rather than merely talk about it.
2. They are close to the customer; they have an almost fanatical dedication to pleasing their clients. In addition, top management knows firsthand what is going on at the frontlines.
3. They value autonomy and entrepreneurship; they encourage their employees in countless ways to innovate.
4. They believe passionately in productivity through people, that unless their employees are respected as the main asset of the company, they cannot work effectively.
5. These excellent corporations are "hands-on value driven." They hold firmly at the core and promote unashamedly explicit overriding values, such as faith in people, service, and quality. These are answers to the question, What does the company stand for? Though everything else changes, these values do not. Hands on means that top management inculcates these values by ceaseless interaction with all sectors of the company.
6. They "stick to the knitting." They branch out into other fields cautiously, if at all, and diversify around their single skill. (I am reminded of a motto one public elementary school put at the bottom of its stationery that reflects this principle: "We only do one thing at Dickinson. EDUCATION. And we do it right.")
7. Despite their complexity, excellent corporations maintain a simple form and a lean staff. They are aware that all employees need to understand the organization clearly if it is to be meaningful in their work and commanding of their loyalty. Violation of this principle generates staffers whose power depends on keeping things unclear.
8. Excellent corporations exhibit simultaneous "loose-tight" properties. Peters and Waterman suggest a classroom analogy: the effective classroom is one, they say, in which discipline is sure and all understand that tardiness is unacceptable and homework is due and will be evaluated. At the same time, this climate allows the teacher to individualize responses to each student.

That these attributes could apply to the analysis of school organization struck me as I reflected on my experiences teaching ninth-grade math and physical science in two socioeconomically different high schools in the late 1960s. One school was a private urban academy oriented toward college preparation. It enrolled approximately 1,000 males, almost all of whom were white and whose parents parted with significant sums of money to have them attend. The other was a public high school in the black ghetto of another big city. Enrollment was about 1,700 males and females, most of whom were low-income and all of whom were black. These schools were different essentially in terms of the population they served. The ways the schools themselves were organized, however, were virtually identical. Each had an extensive array of rules about what could not be done. Each had the typical principal-department form of administration. In each the faculty labored in their self-contained classrooms and interacted little. There was little sense of a collaborative enterprise prompted by involving the people on the line, that is, the teachers, in decision making or curriculum building. Both institutions were hierarchical in the extreme. In neither school was there the ethos of close relationships with the parents. The principals were most likely to have these interactions, usually prompted by a discipline problem.

The similarities continued. In the inner-city school, teachers were left more on their own—which might be a partial precondition for innovation—but in neither case was there any positive encouragement for innovation or experimentation. Both administrations "supervised" the faculty by inspecting their lesson plan books; there was little other on-the-job administrative contact. The central sense of purpose, the overriding value of what the school was for, was present to a degree in the first school, because it was a religious institution, but in neither case was this sense of purpose promulgated through significant interaction between management and all other sectors of the organization. And when administrators might try to interact with faculty and students on a rare occasion, the effect could be ludicrous. I recall the vice-principal of the inner-city school, a well-intentioned but straitlaced middle-aged woman, giving a bizarre little homily over the public address system during morning homeroom. "Now, students," she would shout, "let's make this the finest school in America! We can *do* it! First, there is to be no gum-chewing in the building. Second, the teachers must remember to draw the shades exactly halfway down before they leave in the afternoon. We don't want our school to look unkempt!" By this time the students would be rolling in the aisles with laughter, and another day of chaos would be under way. I will give her some credit, however, for visiting my classroom on two or three occasions, talking to students, and giving me some encouragement. No other administrator ever did any of these things.

In a school, sticking to the knitting refers to the singlemindedness of the entire staff about their shared enterprise, despite distractions and expectations of the organization that it was not originally intended to meet. Historically, our public schools have been expected to cure society's ills:

> Whether in the early nineteenth century or the late twentieth century, Americans have argued for more schooling on the grounds that it would preserve democracy, eliminate poverty, reduce unemployment, ease the assimilation of immigrants to the nation, overcome differences between ethnic groups, advance scientific and technological progress, prevent traffic accidents, raise health standards, refine moral character, and guide young people into useful occupations. (Ravitch, 1983, p. xii)

In practical terms these expectations have resulted in driver education, health checks, free lunches and breakfasts, vocational education programs, school social workers, psychologists, counselors, and other crisis interveners. The ghetto school, being public and serving a low-income population, was particularly susceptible to administrative distraction toward these programs.

The adage that an organization must have a simple form and a lean staff does differentiate these two schools I described, because one school, as a private academy, was much more autonomous, while the other was part of an enormous and complicated urban system. The management of the second included about two dozen full-time employees to handle truancy and discipline problems. While I was not privy to the relationships between the inner-city school's management people and downtown administrators, I was aware of the difficulty of doing anything innovative, from purchasing equipment or materials—even renting a film—to going out of the building with students, because of policies imposed by the central office. The simultaneous loose-tight properties mentioned by Peters and Waterman did not appear to exist in any real sense in either school, however, because of the top-down (machine) nature of their management.

I have spent some time comparing these schools because their very similarity is typical across the nation. The organizational model of rational control worked when its clientele of middle-class youth perceived that the service it rendered was worth whatever pain or boredom it created. Applying this traditional model to black street-wise children was an utter failure. A small portion of the students and a few faculty were the college preparatory section, while the vast majority bided their time or walked the streets every other day. The imposition of the traditional model of schooling in the latter case was a classic example of organizational maladaptation. Even if I had had great expectations of whichever students showed up on a given day or hour,

I could not but have failed completely in that environment. The way the school was set up was all wrong. Each student should have been in a program one-fifth that size, which was individualized, where remediation, enrichment, and counseling opportunities were amply available—where, in short, each student was known and treated as a unique person.

In the final analysis, however, we should apply the Peters and Waterman findings to schools with caution. The large organizations they studied were businesses, oriented toward manufacturing and marketing products and, in some cases, services. Yet to conceive of schools as marketing a product or a service is to fall into a serious trap. The active involvement of parents and especially students in producing learning is essential. The service delivery concept can lull parents and students into a passive stance with regard to education as something done to or for them, such as a haircut or a house-painting job. They pay for it with their taxes, and it is done for them. Many community organizing strategies implicitly held this view as they confronted school officials, but the view of parents and students as consumers is off the mark. It is clear that there must be a partnership among the local actors: school staff, especially principal and teachers, and parents and students. These latter must help deliver the service.

THE LIMITS OF THE PARTNERSHIP MODEL

David Seeley (1981), a former director of New York City's Public Education Association, has proposed a partnership model between school and home that would overcome the distancing tendencies of bureaucracy. Assuming that large school systems as such will not soon atrophy and disappear despite some experiments in decentralization, he argues for the creation of opportunities for *voice* (the capacity for meaningful input by parents and students in school policy and operation) and *choice* (the provision of educational options for parents and students, not only in programs within schools but also among schools themselves). Opportunities for voice and choice will lead to the loyalty of parents and students to these schools, an essential third ingredient in the effective partnership triad.

An example of voice that never fulfilled its potential was the community control experiment in three demonstration districts in New York City in the late 1960s. The resultant decentralization of the city's system into 32 districts with locally elected community school boards did not represent a chance for voice for a sufficient number of parents and students. In Seeley's view, all parents and students should have the opportunity for direct input, rather than being heard merely through representatives.

An instance of choice was shown by the Alum Rock, California, voucher experiment, beginning in 1972. Alum Rock, a school district of 15,000 students near San Francisco, received a federal grant to enable students to choose which school they wished to attend. Although choice was restricted to public schools, allowing them to retain their monopoly, it did encourage an increase in teacher innovation in that they, instead of the central office, controlled use of compensatory funds.

Each of these experiments was flawed, according to Seeley, because it represented only part of the partnership model. Neither voice nor choice by itself was sufficient. Both must be present to produce the loyalty of parents and students. Seeley's approach leaves the reader unsatisfied, however, not because he is wrong but because he is subtly utopian. His critical analysis of the dysfunctions of modern schooling is outstanding, and his proposed realignment of relations between educators and their "clients" is to the point. The problem, of course, is how to bring this state of affairs into being, especially in have-not neighborhoods where choice is nonexistent. In his epilogue he opts for a voucher system as a quick remedy, no matter how politically unrealistic it may be. Although at least two big city systems, Minneapolis and Indianapolis, provide choices in schools for students, no truly free-market plan allowing private schools to compete with public ones has been implemented to date.

But voucher plans, however they are presented, are not the answer for have-nots. Even if federal subsidies went only to low-income parents, presumably allowing them choice between public and private schools, a fundamental problem remains. Here is the argument: if parents choose their local public school, nothing has changed except that the system is free to substitute federal funds for local taxes. If parents choose private schools (assuming there is or will be enough room to accommodate them), they are still at great risk. Basic education is not a commodity for the free market; it is essential for every citizen in order to promote civilization and the common good. Government carries the obligation to provide education for everyone, just as it provides at appropriate levels for public order and the common defense. If low-income people "vote with their feet" to abandon public schools, then private schools they attend will become heavily dependent upon federal (not state and local) funds. These schools will, in effect, become the new public schools for the poor, except they will be funded by a much more tenuous, capricious, politically unstable source. A conservative federal administration wishing to wash its hands of responsibility for support of domestic programs would be in an advantageous position to abandon have-not education altogether. The last state of these poor will be worse than the first. Have-nots must demand change in their present public schools. Vouchers are the siren calling the oppressed to the rocks of destruction.

In the final analysis, David Seeley's partnership concept emphasizes choice at the expense of voice. Thus, it minimizes the political conflict inherent between a professionalized bureaucracy on the one hand and a lay public that is disenfranchised and conditioned to behave as consumers on the other hand. A school-community partnership built through neighborhood organizing is likely to be tense at best, because it will be a power struggle, though not in a conventional sense.

POWER AND THE LIMITS OF A THIRD-PARTY MODEL

The Alinsky legacy of community organizing reminds us that organizing to realign power relations requires the support or aid of third parties. Schools are a natural institution against which to organize disenfranchised parents and students, because these latter have a significant stake in the institution. In their analysis of poor people's movements, Frances Fox Piven and Richard Cloward (1977) pointed out that for a movement against an oppressive institution to be successful, the people themselves must somehow contribute to that institution's existence and operation; that is, they must have an investment in it. But Piven and Cloward cautioned that third parties, governmental or other, can make or break their chances. The following case is an instance of an attempt initiated by a third party to realign power relations among the actors of two elementary inner-city schools in New Haven, Connecticut. The third party in this instance was the Yale University Child Study Center, directed by Dr. James Comer (1980). The King-Baldwin School Project was a five-year-long program dedicated to creating trusting working relationships between home and school within a mental health perspective rather than by piecemeal innovation. As trusting and respectful relations were built and maintained among staff, parents, and students, it was the project's central hypothesis that academic achievement, behavioral improvement, and social skill development would result. Yet Comer did not believe that the skills necessary to bring about such improved relations existed in the current group of staff and parents, hence the rationale for intervention by the third party.

To his credit, Comer did not advocate a simplistic adherence to making school people more caring and more willing to work harder. His analysis of how best to intervene was based on his view of the erosion of the socializing power of the family and the school in our society. For better or worse, he claimed, a small circle of people held social, psychological, economic, and spiritual power over a given child prior to 1940. That was an era of close-knit community, uncomplicated by electronic information networks, raised expectations and skill levels, and the stress and alienation of modern times. The principal of a school was the authority, backed by teachers and parents in a relatively closed and tight social network. Children had fewer decisions to make on their own because electronic media and urban sprawl had not yet begun to broaden their horizons. "We are not a nation of people in daily contact with strangers," Comer wrote (1980, p. 12), recognizing a stark fact that underlies the opportunity children have today to make more decisions on their own despite their being no more mature than their forebears at the same age.

The typical school today forges ahead as if nothing had changed in the past fifty years. The principal still attempts to be autocratic, yet is, in fact, powerless, said Comer. The way back to regaining power is not, therefore, to call for more authoritarian behavior by the principal or a return to the basics. To do so is to miss the real sources of socializing power in modern society. Rather, the struggle is to rebuild community within the school setting in a new way. Comer suggested that this is best accomplished by a governance structure that reflects the diverse needs of the actors and through which they can all participate in the school process—have voice, in Seeley's terms. In this respect, though, Comer goes beyond Seeley, who did not see his partnership model as a form of governance structure. Leadership, exerted especially through the principal's role, must be grounded in "human relations, child development, and organizational theory" (p. 40). Comer, with these phrases, asked principals to become humanistic managers who build and maintain consensus on a foundation of trust and mutual respect through shared power. Romantic though this scenario appears, it is the necessary antidote for the disruptive student behavior in inner-city schools. Student disruption makes educators defensive and parents embarrassed and angry; it is a principal source of conflict between adults in such schools. Parents blame teachers for not making their children behave, attributing this failure to racism. Educators react by blaming parents for not preparing their children for school.

Comer decries confrontation as a tactic in school reform; he sees it as only adding fuel to the fire. The way back to community is through establishment of cooperative forms of participation in schools, admittedly a most difficult task. In Comer's model, an expert third party intervened in the form of a demonstration project whose overall objectives were to involve all adults in the school program so that they would come to know one another as persons rather than as stereotypes, to help teachers and parents through workshops and other means to increase their skills in dealing with the children, and to aid the educational staff in improving the curriculum.

The King-Baldwin School Project cost $2.615 million over six years and significantly boosted achievement scores of the children in these schools over other Title I schools in New Haven between 1969 and 1979. Fifty-five percent of the funds paid professional salaries (that is, Child Study Center personnel) and 35–40 percent went for parent or teacher stipends. While over $260,000 per school per year is an unreasonable expenditure to expect for any given school except on a demonstration basis, the intervention project did develop some transportable features that would not necessarily cost much to implement. A school governance body consisting of principal, teachers, staff, and parent representatives is certainly economically feasible. The use of talented teachers—and there are always such individuals even in the most troubled schools—to develop curriculum innovations could be encouraged without great cost. Comer warned, though, that the mental health aspect of the program ought to be carried out by outside professionals, since it is unlikely that insiders will possess the requisite skills. There must also be long-term commitment to the project by the school system itself so that when the inevitable conflicts occur, the system does not abandon the project and let it die.

There are obvious problems with the third-party model, however. The most obvious is that it was very expensive; in this respect it is no model at all—in the sense of being able to be duplicated. Less obvious is that it was initiated by a third party, in this case Yale's Child Study Center. Third-party initiation poses two problems. First, school people have every reason to wonder about the motives of these professionals. Their suspicion in this example was only gradually worn away during the early years by the persistence of the project directors and by the opportunity to gain increased power (sense of control) in the school by all concerned. What they said they would do, for the most part the professionals did. Second, we might assume from this case that no school reform can be accomplished unless some benevolent outside institution, like a deus ex machina, comes from nowhere to promote the reform. The model says nothing about how local school participants, especially parents, could organize themselves for such reform. Comer does not preclude this possibility, but his experience did not contain the know-how for "organizing ourselves." His anxiety over confrontational tactics leads us to believe they are pointless and destructive; but one should not conclude that they are always counter-productive, even though much conflict in the recent history of urban education has failed to lead to program improvement, because power relations were not affected.

Comer's study provides us with insight into how much work is required to establish cooperative interaction and how much further work is needed to sustain it. Time, energy, and tolerance for failure are essential ingredients, but they are not sufficient by themselves. Human relations skills must be taught and modeled. Enhanced management skills, by the principal, by teachers in the classrooms, by parents in their school involvement and with their children at home, are the goal, which will not be reached without training by people who know how to do it. Finally, this approach demands that every aspect of the school be subject to change; it must be holistic, not piecemeal.

Comer seemed correct in anticipating that teacher unions, central office, and other outside powers would not object to sharing power in the long run if the project actually improved the working conditions of teachers and the achievement of children. But I missed the sense of profound alienation and distrust present in most inner-city schools, and reflected in so many first-person accounts and other writings about them. How does the reformer overcome this suspicion that, almost by definition, must exist in the troubled school setting? Comer said little about the origins of his project except that initial negotiations included the superintendent. There also can be no question that the immense prestige and fund-raising potential of the Yale University name gave instant credibility to the proposal. In short, the union, the PTA, central office, or the board will be unlikely to give support to a power-sharing proposal merely because someone suggests it and points to the New Haven project as the model. Comer's project report offers many sophisticated tips on possible program components once it is under way, and his analysis of the loss of power of the formerly close social network surrounding the child as the origin of much child misbehavior is also consistent and helpful. But Comer's analysis fails to come to grips with how people can create the circumstances that enable them to share power. In his project, poor people had the school improved for them once again by the professionals. Can they do it themselves, or with much less leadership from professionals?

TABLE 4.2
STRENGTHS AND LIMITATIONS
OF
REFORM MODELS

MODEL	STRENGTHS	LIMITATIONS
PACKAGED INNOVATION (REFORM-FROM-WITHIN)	Program innovations can boost morale, sometimes alter institutional processes.	Model does not deal with cultural beliefs and modal regularities of the professional bureaucracy. It does not involve the "client."
EXCELLENT CORPORATION	It provides a model of service and sensitivity to market, promotes internal cohesion and autonomy simultaneously.	The model promotes a service delivery concept of education, making parents and students into passive consumers.
PARTNERSHIP	This model promotes close working relationships between home and school through voice, choice, and loyalty.	The model provides no strategy for creating this partnership. It is not a governance model.
THIRD PARTY (MENTAL HEALTH)	The model takes a holistic approach to change. It seeks equalization of power relations among all actors. It includes a governance function for "clients."	It avoids confrontation and requires considerable funding. It does not seek community empowerment as such with regard to school, relying instead on third-party expertise.
RESPONSIBLE PARTY	This model suggests a politically feasible governance model.	It does not suggest how to achieve the model if school officials resist.

THE RESPONSIBLE PARTY MODEL

The models thus far presented suffer from a common weakness: failure to provide the means to empower parents, students, and other community members with regard to dealing with their schools. Even Comer's third-party model, although it establishes a governance structure of school personnel and parents, relies heavily on outside (mental health) expertise to bring this structure into being and maintain it. An elaboration of the concept of this structure, which would include all sectors interested in the school, is the responsible party model, proposed by Joyce, Hersh, and McKibbin (1983). These collaborative local governance groups would include representatives from five sectors:

1. General public
2. Site and district administrators
3. Teachers
4. Technical consultants
5. "Patrons of the school": parents and students.

Including district administrators and technical consultants in the group would allay fears that granting such groups policymaking powers would lead to the creation of deviant institutional configurations and destroy the power of central office over local schools. Such local governance has the potential to avoid the negative results of loose-coupling, whereby little supervision and accountability can occur. The BUILD Academy of Buffalo, New York, to be discussed in Chapter 6, is an example of the success resulting from this increased inclusion (Brown, 1978).

Table 4.2 summarizes the strengths and limitations of the models discussed in the chapter.

This book suggests that neighborhood organizations in inner-city neighborhoods can organize to establish these governance bodies. The main thrust of the neighborhood organization is to get the school under control—though not under *its* control—and in doing so to create a new climate and mechanisms whereby its membership, especially parents and students, can gain increased voice in the school operation.

Chapters to follow examine the history of citizen involvement in schools, the nature of the contemporary neighborhood organization, ways in which it can create linkages with local schools for reform purposes, and issues to be dealt with as organizing begins and continues.

5

Forerunners of Citizen
Influence in Education

*Organized parents are learning to wield political power in
order to exert greater parental influence in school affairs.
(Weinberg, 1983, p. 246)*

Developments in cities and their educational systems have profoundly influenced the ways in which parents and other citizens could
participate in the educational process. The history of citizen involvement is, then, closely tied to several currents in American history since
the country began to industrialize in the early nineteenth century.
Rapid urbanization, the struggle of blacks for equality, and the later
decline of the central city within the shell of the metropolis each saw
unique efforts by citizens to affect their children's education.

This chapter discusses forms of citizen participation relevant to
education during the century and a half preceding the upheavals of the
1960s. The development and mutation of bureaucratic forms of governing urban schools, a basically localized process, paralleled changes
in municipal government itself. Citizen involvement was also localized
and most often took the form of reaction to school policy decisions.
The latter part of this period is notable for the arrival of two divergent
approaches to organizing for social reform, namely, social work and
political activism, rooted in two opposing ideologies. Although parents
were hardly ever galvanized into an organized political force as potent
as those within the system, they continuously conducted sorties against
the citadels of education.

THE ORIGINS OF BUREAUCRACY
IN THE DECLINE OF VOLUNTARISM

During the first half of the nineteenth century, before the peak of
Horace Mann's influence on behalf of the common school, education

in cities took place largely in schools administered by self-appointed "first citizens," who saw their efforts as the obligation for responsible action due to their high social station. These schools were of three types:

1. Proprietary, in which the teacher was the paid tutor of the group
2. Incorporated by the state yet governed by private trustees, the forerunners of academies and colleges, or
3. Charity schools for the poor, sponsored by churches (Tyack, 1981)

The New York Free School Society incorporated some of these forms in ministering to thousands of elementary-aged children during the early nineteenth century (Katz, 1973).

This model of paternalistic voluntarism fit the mercantile, preindustrial city. Although the New York Free School Society operated several schools, it did not utilize the elaborate organization or professional control that we ordinarily associate with contemporary schooling. A variant of this model, corporate voluntarism, focused primarily on high school or college-level education. It was termed corporate because the administrative control applied to single, incorporated educational institutions, but again the control was exerted by the elite of the citizenry, even though in some cases tax money supported the institution.

Even as early as 1820, however, there were some local residents who objected to this undemocratic monopoly of power. They were part of a generalized attack on monopolies that characterized the public values of this period. *Democratic localism*, as it later came to be known, represented a countervailing organizational form rooted in the rural community school. It not only opposed paternalistic voluntarism, but also opposed any bureaucratic tendencies toward centralization and professionalization.

Under democratic localism, which was essentially a rural phenomenon, each local school would be run by elected local boards. This approach flourished for only a brief time, however, since its viewpoint was so inconsistent with the stirrings of urbanization of the time. At its worst, democratic localism was a tyranny of local majorities, who sought the dominance of their own narrow sectarian or political bias in the school. At its best it held the potential for a liberalizing education uncharacteristic of the schools of this or later periods (Katz, 1973).

As mid-nineteenth century cities began to experience industriali-
zation, that is, the organization of production into factories wherein
workers endlessly repeated the same simplified task, education under-
went incipient bureaucratization. The upper classes had traditionally
employed education as a means of civilizing the lower classes. They
now perceived centralized administration of schooling and standardization of curriculum and procedure as the modern way to avoid the
despotic tendencies of democratic localism as well as to accomplish
the task of education of the masses in the most efficient manner. The
concept drew even wider public acceptance because it afforded some
measure of public accountability.

THE RIGID BUREAUCRACY

In the quarter century after the Civil War, cities were filling up
with the first waves of immigrants from southern and eastern Europe.
New technologies, particularly the steam engine, fed the growth of
factories; these clamorous workplaces became the focal points of
cities, the centers of residential neighborhoods. As the turn of the
century approached, cities were annexing land voraciously and building roads, bridges, docks, and sewers. The capital required for all this
development spawned a peculiar form of governmental machinery to
generate it: the boss system. Founded on ward patronage and lending
itself to corrupt practice, the boss system endured because most observers saw it as the only practical way to govern the unruly polyglot
throngs of the cities.

During this period the bureaucratic systematization of education
spread throughout urban America. But these early school bureaucracies were far more rigid and inflexible than those we know today. For
example, Superintendent Samuel King, appointed in 1874 to oversee a
system with 1,168 students in Portland, Oregon, not only sought precise control of every activity of student and teacher alike, but also was
one of the first educators in the nation to give achievement tests and
publish the results in the city's newspaper, with each child's score and
school next to his or her name (Tyack, 1973). A vast proportion failed
the test. Not surprisingly, teachers joined irate parents to force King's
resignation a short time later.

The bureaucratization of Portland's schools was to continue until a
report critical of this practice was issued by Ellwood P. Cubberly in
1913. The rigidity of the system, like that of many others in America,
was evident in a remark by a later superintendent to the effect that he

saw the system as functioning at its best when he could tell at a given hour what page in the same textbook every child would be working on. There was criticism from the public of such ironclad drill, which was grounded in a deeper suspicion of the changes wrought by centralization and professionalism, but it had little effect on the direction of education during these decades.

Two other developments concerning citizen participation during this period deserve mention. First, blacks in some places acted immediately after the Civil War to protest against segregated schools. Black parents led a successful school boycott in Chicago in 1865 and an unsuccessful one in Buffalo in 1867 (Meier & Rudwick, 1973). A second development, not directly related to education, was the emergence of neighborhood improvement associations in the new suburbs (Fisher, 1984). Dedicated to neighborhood maintenance, these conservative associations sought to protect upper-class property values and prerogatives. An early example, in Woodlawn outside Chicago, was the Woodlawn Improvement Association, which was created in 1882. Eight decades later, after Woodlawn had been annexed by the city and had become a black ghetto, it was to be the setting for one of the most famous community organizations in the United States, The Woodlawn Organization (TWO), a radical-activist form of citizen participation. Nonetheless, neighborhood improvement associations have persisted to the present and have frequently lent their weight to residents involved in school issues.

THE LOOSE BUREAUCRACY AND ELITE CONTROL

At the turn of the century, public reaction to the injustices of both the factory and the factory-like school were finding voice in the theories of Progressivism. A new kind of corporate captain began to emerge, a liberal concerned about the stress placed on urban communities by the crowding in of foreign-born workers. Spurred by the growing legitimacy of social science, professionalism became the watchword in social service. Two specific organizational forms embodied this liberal reform thrust: the settlement house and the school as community center.

Drawing on the model of Toynbee Hall, established in the slums of London in 1886, where Oxford students lived for a time to minister to the needs of the poor, groups of upper-class citizens began establishing similar settlement houses in American cities. The first such settlement house, the Neighborhood Guild in New York City, was established in 1886 by Stanton Coit (Violas, 1978). The best known was Chicago's Hull House, founded by Jane Addams and Ellen Gates Starr in 1906. By 1911, there were more than 400 urban settlement houses mediating the social distance between the rich and the poor. The emphasis was on community, not class, in this new liberal context. Organizing to help the poor meant working within the existing power structure, not against it, an idea central to the social work approach.

The school as community center represented another adaptation of this view. According to one historian, there were actually four distinct periods of activity around this concept (Wayland, 1958). The first, minor interest at the turn of the century led to the second, a strong movement from World War I to 1925 to use school facilities to meet adult social service needs in, for example, health and nutrition education. By 1920, school community centers existed in 107 American cities (Fisher, 1984). The 1935 C. S. Mott Foundation experiment, which included curriculum innovations for children and entertainment as well as social services for adults and children alike, began the third period of viewing the school as a community center. By 1950, a number of officially sponsored studies assessed the impact of the Mott Community School Plan, which by then had reached more than fifty cities. What had been experimental in the third period had become a matter of course in the fourth.

Schools as community centers differed from settlement houses, however, in that they were publicly funded and allowed for neighborhood citizen representatives on their governing boards. The settlement houses were governed by the rich, who did not live in the neighborhood. The distance between the organizing institution and the people organized narrowed under the community school concept (Hatton, 1979).

In many cities the demand for reform of boss government and ward-based politics led to the introduction of the weak-mayor system, in which the executive functions were carried out by a professional manager hired by the city council. In addition, home-rule legislation in several states allowed cities to have more say in their own affairs. Prior to this time cities were required to ask permission of the state for the smallest changes, even the renaming of alleys.

"Centralization," "expertise," "professionalism," "efficiency," and "nonpolitical" now adorned the colors of reform in education. Schools in large cities, now vast admixtures of ethnic subcultures, appeared ungovernable without new systematic approaches that allowed for the autonomy of professional educators yet provided the control of centralized administration. The result in most cases was a more loosely coupled bureaucracy, the forerunner of today's urban education systems.

Revisionist historians, such as Michael Katz, Joel Spring, and Paul Violas, have seen the bureaucratization and professionalization of education as a deliberate attempt to mold the attitudes of the working class, including blacks, for adaptation to the dull tasks of factory life. The school as community center, like the settlement house movement before it, paralleled formal schooling in its emphasis on programs that stressed Americanization (the melting-pot theme), citizenship, and docility to group values. According to Violas (1978), major educational innovations that enhanced this attitude were compulsory school attendance laws (Mississippi was the last state to adopt such a law, in 1918), the play movement, student extracurricular activities, vocational training and guidance, and the emergence of the professional school administrator.[1]

Some ethnic working-class people informally resisted this liberal pressure to "melt." School truancy rates were high, although they were high among the middle class as well (Violas, 1978). Radical leftists opposed the growing plutocratic control of education by establishing alternative schools in New York and New Jersey, drawing especially on the growing strength of the American labor movement (Spring, 1972).

Blacks resisted the pressure on them to attend segregated schools, many of which were devoted exclusively to industrial training. The postwar period witnessed a wave of school boycotts by blacks, the most intense of which occurred in Springfield, Ohio, during 1922 and 1923 (Meier & Rudwick, 1973). When the school board there decided to make a previously integrated school, Fulton, an "all-Negro" elementary school, the black parents organized a boycott and picketed throughout the entire year. Two elements of this action are notable: First, the board had hired twelve black teachers to staff the school, the first such teachers in more than forty years. As a result of the boycott, however, the board fired them all the next year, even though their credentials and experience put them well above the minimum. The parents' outrage at the racism of the school policy decision could not be assuaged by the seemingly enlightened action to finally hire blacks as teachers. The board and its successors showed their true inclinations by not hiring any more black teachers for another twenty-five years. Second, the community organization that truly dominated the school board was seen to be the segregationist Ku Klux Klan. The school superintendent openly belonged to it. Although the local court disallowed assignment of children to schools by race, white principals at all other Springfield schools would not enroll black children in their schools, but they did enroll whites from Fulton. Thus, Fulton became

97 percent black the next year. When the community organization's efforts are opposed by the broader community, they are much less likely to succeed, despite support of powerful third parties.

Thus it was that in the fifty years prior to the Great Depression, the predominant form of community organizing was that which was done to the community by powerful outsiders who sought to shape it to their conceptions of middle-class virtue intertwined with working-class docility. The small number of instances of resistance to the growing control of urban school systems by the new elite credo of professionalism and centralization, covertly reinforcing classism and racism, implies that these controls were highly successful. The new insulation of the urban system bureaucrats made them unaccountable to their constituents, and the national core culture had not shifted to support these have-not groups. However, the Depression years would dislocate this core, prompting a tradition of more sympathy for have-nots and of government intervention on their behalf.

THE RISE OF RADICAL ORGANIZING

From 1930 to 1945, the country's economy dropped precipitously into the Great Depression and "roller-coastered" upward through the Second World War. The urban centers were first devastated by unemployment, then revivified by the industrial demands of war. President Franklin Delano Roosevelt, whose trickle-down economic theories did not work during his first term, initiated a second New Deal more in accord with the country's demand that the federal government do something to alleviate its suffering. A spate of legislative actions in mid-decade involved the federal government in American life to a depth never before seen. From Social Security to the Rural Electrification Administration, mechanisms were created to deal directly with social stress.

Important for our purposes are the Wagner Act of 1935, which legitimized and protected collective bargaining by unions, and the Civilian Conservation Corps (CCC). In the former case, the government lent support to what had been radical grassroots labor organizing. In the latter, a program to provide work relief for unemployed youth, the federal government drew closer to official intervention in education, although it had begun funding public secondary programs in vocational education in 1917 after passage of the Smith-Hughes Act. The CCC was a program that served essentially the same educational goals for the working class as did the public schools: training youth in docility and "industrial realism" (Violas, 1978, p. 233).

Two developments, one at the beginning of the decade of the 1930s and the other at its end, justifiably allow this period to be considered the radical era of community organizing. Although these organizing activities were not directed specifically at schools, whose centralization and professionalization were now virtually complete and unchallenged, they began the tradition of community pressure exerted by a mass-based, multi-issue organization whose goals are the redistribution of resources and the improvement of local service delivery. Lessons learned during these years would be applied to the upheavals of the 1960s.

Early in the decade, the Communist Party (CPUSA) successfully organized the urban unemployed on the issues of relief, housing, and race discrimination (Naison, 1981). CPUSA organizers were particularly effective in Harlem during these early years because they concentrated on the neighborhood as the focal point for their efforts. After 1937, however, CPUSA began to hew to the Moscow line of emphasis on international issues. It thereby lost credibility with local residents, whom it neglected in favor of translocal issues.

Union organizing, also a fertile field for the CPUSA, gave rise to the second development, the appearance of Saul D. Alinsky, a union organizer himself and a trained criminologist, who forged the Back of the Yards Neighborhood Council in a multiethnic slum on the south side of Chicago. This group of resident leaders, such as priests and labor chiefs, began to agitate for betterment of the neighborhood on such vital matters as jobs, improved wages, upgraded housing, and an end to retail price gouging by storeowners. Using pressure tactics, coupled with behind-the-scenes negotiations, Alinsky's group gained a string of victories and national name for him. He went on to organize similar coalitions in other large cities until his death in 1972. If this was the period of the blossoming of the radical view of political activism, a view in which the community is a power base, then Saul Alinsky was its preeminent political activist.

Progress of the Back of the Yards Council held a bittersweet outcome, however (Alinsky, 1972a). By 1950, after many victories and an improved standard of living for many of its 200,000 residents, the area's whites (Poles, Slovaks, Germans, and Lithuanians) had overcome their old enmities and united against the blacks and Mexicans of the neighborhoods, making them community scapegoats. In moving out of poverty they had taken on the prejudices of the middle class; political activism had been only partially successful.

American education had now seen, in one hundred years' time, a massive shift from an agrarian-oriented, volunteer-controlled miscellany of schools to large, centralized bureaucratic systems in densely populated urban centers, hubs of industry and commerce. Elite citizens' traditional concerns with the education of the masses had remained, although their perceptions of what this concept meant had shifted with the times. Uncoordinated private charity toward the poor had given way to public policy aimed at fitting the working class to its destiny of physical labor.

The radical revisionists' conception of a conspiracy of the wealthy to numb the lower classes toward factory work, while giving the illusion of upward mobility through schooling, may be open to question. Some groups of Jews, Chinese, and Japanese were able to adapt to the schools of the early twentieth century, using them to move into white-collar jobs in significant numbers, though it is a point of controversy whether they had improved their economic position before they did or as a result of doing so (Berube, 1984). For most others of the lower classes, however, the fact remained that urban schools served their dreams of economic success poorly, if at all. There is also sufficient evidence that many educational leaders sought social control as their principal objective. Many still do.

In becoming systematically organized, schools had become pathologically insulated from their communities, especially those of the working classes. But the social ferment of the 1930s in the nation's factories and neighborhoods would form the pattern for dissent in the 1960s, when the civil rights movement would awaken America to poverty in new ways.

By 1940, two views of community organizing were in place, ready to clash in the social arena. The social work approach saw low-income residents as unable to overcome their problems without the intervention and leadership of the middle class, particularly social work professionals. It harked back to a time of noblesse oblige, the duty of the elite citizenry for social responsibility inherent in their high station. In this view, the victims of poverty are themselves blamed, rather than the economic and political systems that created their poverty. It therefore did not admit the poor into the decision-making processes affecting them. It sought instead to fit the have-not into a group mindset, generated by the social worker. Self-determination from this perspective meant self-chosen adaptation; those among the poor who enthusiastically accepted plutocratic objectives and emulated their perspective and behaviors were considered leaders.[2]

The social work approach to community organizing, the life-force of settlement house activity around 1910 and schools as community centers a decade after, was reinvigorated in the C. S. Mott Foundation funding of the Flint Community School Program in 1935. The idea was not much different from the school as community center: Professional social workers identified neighborhood social needs and resources and used the school as a staging area for programs to meet these needs, but in this plan residents were given a role in program design, albeit one extremely limited in authority (Hatton, 1979).

Political activism, the polar opposite of the social work approach to community organizing, reacted strenuously against what it saw as professional support of elitist goals and methods. Basing its strength on members of the working class themselves, it blamed systems, not victims, for their misery. It demanded that they be included in policy-making that touched their lives. It was an ideology of conflict and confrontation. Self-determination meant considerable control over the levers of political and economic power by these citizens; its leaders were those who led the charge. Political activism was the antithesis of middle-class ideas of consensus politics.

THE SEEDS OF REVOLUTION

The twenty-year period spanning the end of World War II and the mid-1960s saw drastic changes in central cities, now being hemmed in by suburbs on all sides. Returning servicemen were enabled to buy new homes in suburban tracts, encouraged by the Federal Home Loan Bank Act of 1932 and the Servicemen's Readjustment Act of 1944, which made loan terms for returning GIs especially attractive and financed suburban housing starts. Cheap gasoline and natural gas made large homes accessible and comfortable even as government was ignoring low-income family rental needs in cities. The Federal Aid Highway Act of 1956 subsidized the interstate highway system, which chopped up inner-city neighborhoods and provided transit to the suburbs. The net result of these and other federal policies was the decline of central cities, particularly those in northern industrial areas.[3]

Changes in cities reflected growing geographic segregation between whites and blacks. Neighborhood organizing during this era was predominantly conservative, although as early as 1953, urban have-nots began to collectively resist "urban renewal," which was resulting in the demolition of their aging neighborhoods (Marciniak, 1981). The Civic Clubs of Houston, which constitute a classic example of this national conservatism, were formed in 1948 to promote and defend homeowners' property values, since that city has never controlled land use by zoning. Even though neighborhood groups were reactionary and racist, employing deed restrictions in lieu of zoning, they also became divisive of their own residents. Not everyone agreed with the leaders' policies on criteria for neighborhood maintenance, for example (Fisher, 1984).

Another instance of conservative neighborhood organizing was related to the shift in the United States to a war economy as a basis for prosperity. Whole communities sprang up around the new defense industries in the South. The social problems instigated by this massive social dislocation were to be addressed by the United Community Defense Service (UCDS), whose approach resembled the old community school concept (Fisher, 1984).

This Cold War era continued to see citizen attempts to influence education policy, though. In 1949, for example, a citywide citizens' coalition in New York City, the Public Education Association, joined with Teachers College and the New York Board of Education to begin the Bronx Park Community Project as a step toward community control of schools (LaNoue & Smith, 1971). A survey of 217 superintendents in Massachusetts in 1952 reported that 90 percent experienced pressure from parent groups, though these groups appeared about evenly split between those protesting innovations and those demanding them (Gross, 1958).

The major landmark with regard to schools during these two decades, however, occurred in 1954 when the U.S. Supreme Court ruled that separate but equal schools for blacks were unconstitutional. A year later, the Court required that all school districts in the country desegregate "with all deliberate speed," but with few exceptions, none did for at least another decade. This case highlights both the strength and weakness of litigation as a strategy on behalf of the disenfranchised. On the one hand, the NAACP had used the lawsuit to redress blacks' grievances against segregation for almost fifty years prior to this victory. And they had won some gains. Litigation had afforded them direct access to power and influence despite its consumption of time and demands for expertise. On the other hand, litigation cannot ensure that the legal remedies granted will be enforced (Davies, 1981). In fact, a great deal of citizen participation since 1954 has been motivated by opposition to desegregation.

Thus, on the eve of the 1960s, history had provided a number of precedents that, when brought together, would increase citizen participation in education, especially by low- and moderate-income residents, to a new level. The federal government had become progressively more active in education. The Smith-Hughes Act of 1917 was a start. New Deal programs provided for the education of the unemployed and for school construction (Ornstein & Levine, 1985). The GI Bill in 1944 allocated federal funds for the continued education of veterans. The Supreme Court's *Brown* decision in 1954 would henceforward enmesh the courts in education. The 1958 National Defense Education Act in reaction to Russia's launching of Sputnik the previous year involved federal funds for curriculum reform in science, math, and foreign language. This deepening involvement by the national government would continue, supporting nationwide experiments in participation by the poor, not only in education but also in many other federally funded activities designed to improve their cities and neighborhoods.

Another factor contributing to the participatory reform ethos of the 1960s was the civil rights movement in the South, which when it was transported to Northern cities with their growing unemployment and black underclass, led to the urban riots of the mid-decade. A third factor was the legacy of radical organizing by urban have-nots, grounded in the labor movement of the Great Depression era. With the help of Saul Alinsky, these residents had learned how to collectively confront the forces that produced and maintained the depressing conditions of their daily existence.

The following chapter explores how the liberal reforms of the 1960s and 1970s created enhanced opportunities for the poor to become more politically involved in the education of their children. These broad reform trends, for the most part based on federal initiatives but flowing also from citizen demands for local control, formed a framework for the development of the contemporary neighborhood organization.

6

The Liberal Legacy
of Citizen Participation
in Education

*If you genuinely seek the means to educational equity for all
our people, you must encourage parent attention to politics as
the greatest instrument of instructional reform extant.
(Edmonds, 1979, p. 37)*

The second half of the twentieth century in the United States
began as a period of rising expectations, both economic and educational. This chapter details how many urban have-nots, particularly
racial minorities, came to see their own participation in political decision making as the best remedy for the decline of their schools. Their
principal ally during this period would be the federal government.

Desegregation was one social movement that nurtured citizen
participation in education, for both progressive and reactionary ends.
Federal funding to improve inner-city schools fostered the development and widespread use of parent or resident advisory councils. The
ethic of participation also took form in a variety of efforts to gain fuller
political influence, if not outright control, over the inner city's schools
by community residents. All three trends cross-fertilized each other to
nurture a new have-not leadership in neighborhoods, people experienced in confrontation yet sophisticated in the political arts of organization building and negotiation.

DESEGREGATION

Desegregation of schools was officially set in motion in the 1954
U.S. Supreme Court *Brown* decision, but the means to achieve it were
not spelled out. The legal thrust of the NAACP for decades had been
to make America a color-blind society, a society in which race made

no difference. The 1955 "Brown II" decision of the Court still left the means of desegregation up to local school authorities, out of deference to the South, even though the Court required that discriminatory practices be ended "with all deliberate speed." This reliance on voluntary compliance ensured that little would be done and gave credibility to an opposing ideology that race should be a factor in social policy. This emphasis on color-consciousness was to become the foundation for government and court decision making on race relations to the present (Ravitch, 1983).

The South had been particularly vulnerable to court actions after 1954 because of its segregationist laws, declared unconstitutional by the *Brown* decision. Beginning at Central High School, in Little Rock, Arkansas, in 1957, confrontations between segregationist and desegregationist forces spread across the South in the next five years, paralleling and abetting the growing civil rights movement begun in 1955 with the Montgomery, Alabama, bus boycott. By 1964, however, still less than 2 percent of the black students in the eleven states of the South were attending school with whites. But in the mid-1960s there came into being two federal weapons that hurried Southern desegregation along, and as a result the 2 percent of black students attending school with whites in the South in 1964 became 91 percent by 1971. The first weapon was the Civil Rights Act of 1964, Title VI, which forbade racial discrimination in federally funded programs. The weapon became fully loaded a year later with the passage of the Elementary and Secondary Education Act (ESEA), which provided federal funds to school districts. The second weapon was a landmark decision in 1967 by Judge John Minor Wisdom of the Fifth Circuit Court of Appeals upholding Department of Health, Education, and Welfare (HEW) guidelines for desegregation plans. Thus were Southern school districts compelled to take affirmative steps to mix students by race, including busing if necessary.

The North differed from the South, however, in its racial demographics as well as its laws. Blacks displaced from Southern farms by agricultural mechanization between 1940 and 1966 had poured into the central cities, principally in the North, doubling their black populations between 1950 and 1966, while white populations remained stable or declined. Concentration of blacks under poverty conditions gave rise among some black leaders to feelings of despair over integrationist goals. They began to lean toward political separatism and to desire control over their own communities. These sentiments were squarely opposed to desegregationist ideology. Nonetheless, integrationists in these communities and in government continued to press for an end to racially isolated schools. During the late 1960s and early 1970s, orders to bus for desegregation purposes became common not only in many large cities of the North and West, from Boston to San Francisco, but also in many smaller cities. However, in the North the real challenge was to the district lines, not to neighborhood school boundaries, because many large cities were already predominantly black. Busing orders in these cities ultimately snagged on the vast distances involved in busing, despite integrationist pressure for a metropolitan strategy that would involve suburbs in cross-district busing plans.

In this liberal time, government was listening to and supporting two seemingly antithetical movements, one integrationist and the other separatist. There was federal support for desegregation, on the one hand, yet there were also funds for programs to improve urban inner-city schools, racially isolated though they were. Such support led in each case to the creation of citizen participation vehicles that moved have-nots closer to political influence in their schools.

Desegregation orders led to three types of citizen participation. The first was the parent or citizen advisory council established by the federal district court to advise the court and monitor the implementation of the plan. Usually these groups were multiethnic in makeup; Boston's Racial Ethnic Parent Council (REPC) was a foremost example. The second type of citizen organization was the formal multiracial or multiethnic coalition formed from grassroots groups to address desegregation issues. Some cities, for example, Detroit, Memphis, and Tulsa, saw these coalitions develop as a result of desegregation orders (Crowfoot et al., 1982). In most cases these associations were focused solely on making desegregation work effectively. For example, the Heights Community Congress was formed in 1971 in two middle-class inner-ring suburbs of Cleveland, Cleveland Heights and University Heights, to oppose resegregation and blockbusting (Davies et al., 1979). It was a federation of church, educational, civic, senior citizen, and government groups that united to press for control of integration in housing and education and to promote electoral change at the municipal level. Their strategy was consensus building with all parties involved, which turned out to be effective for the homogeneously middle-class population.

A third type of citizen organization arose in opposition to desegregation. These coalitions, usually of white, working-class ethnic groups, employed conflict tactics that received disproportionate publicity. One of the best-known examples was ROAR (Restore Our Alienated Rights) in Boston's Charlestown section.[1] Most working-class associations formed during the desegregation period (1965–1975) were, if they were white, opposed to desegregation, or if they were minority, used confrontational tactics with the school system to obtain changes in a variety of areas from organizational procedures to new programming (Crowfoot et al., 1982).

What have been the results of two decades of desegregation? One important result has been the marked decline of racially isolated (where the student population is more than 90 percent minority) schools in the South between 1968 and 1980. In 1968, 78 percent of the schools were racially isolated; in 1980, only 23 percent were (Ornstein & Levine, 1985). With some qualifications, there is considerable evidence that blacks have consistently favored busing for desegregation despite white opposition to it (Weinberg, 1983). Where blacks are critical of busing, they usually have borne an unfair share of the burden for it. Although Mexican-Americans in the Southwest have tended to fall between whites and blacks in their attitudes toward busing for desegregation, they have tended to follow whites in their attitudes toward blacks.

Desegregation in the Northern cities, however, has not been so successful. Where housing patterns separate large groups of minority and white citizens in relatively distant neighborhoods, the number of racially isolated schools has actually increased. In 1968, 43 percent of Northern big-city schools were racially isolated; in 1980, 49 percent were. Although midwestern, western, and border states have all experienced declines in the percentages of these segregated schools, big cities themselves have had to contend with increasingly nonwhite populations. The public school systems in turn saw their nonwhite populations increase in proportion even faster than that of the cities. This intensified resegregation has made the demands for improvement of neighborhood schools—racially isolated minority schools—more urgent.

The majority of studies on the instructional effects of desegregation have focused on the improvement of achievement levels of minority children without paying attention to classroom or intraschool processes (Weinberg, 1983). Overall, with some qualifications, the research evidence indicates that minority students make achievement level gains under desegregation. The greatest gains are made where attention is given to make the education process effective for them, where the school is perceived as fair, and where other effectiveness characteristics interact with each other. Studies have also shown that white students' achievement does not suffer necessarily and that conversational linguistic differences (such as black English vernacular versus Standard English) are readily overcome by both student groups.

What we have chiefly learned, though, from the experience of desegregation is that the mere act of mixing races in schools does not necessarily produce integration, described by Meyer Weinberg (1983) as a "social situation marked by mutual respect and equal dignity in an atmosphere of acceptance and encouragement of distinctive cultural patterns" (p. 172). On the positive side, as we have mentioned, desegregation has promoted academic achievement among minorities and boosted their aspiration and subsequent college enrollment levels. It has also increased interracial interaction and led to acceptance in many communities of desegregation as the ordinary course of events; but there have been many negatives as well. Teachers and administrators have remained prejudiced against minority students; black students have received discriminatory suspensions and expulsions; there has been racially discriminatory placement of minority students in classrooms for the mentally retarded or in ability groups and tracking systems leading to manual labor jobs.

Thus not only is contact important in achieving interracial harmony and justice, but also the context of that interaction—how it is structured—is extremely important. Yet few schools are actively engaged, both procedurally and in matters of curriculum, to bring it about. In view of this lack of attention to effectiveness in the school program, writes Weinberg, "the reality of unformalized school progress is all the more impressive" (1983, p. 189).

Blacks and other minorities who have pressed for desegregation have done so because they wanted to make available to their own people the same educational resources, especially experienced teachers and programs with higher academic expectations, that were available to middle-class whites. Their goal was not merely to promote intergroup enlightenment. Gaining access was not, however, sufficient; the school process had to change as well, as integrationists soon learned. Minority have-nots whose orientation was separatist also focused on school improvement. In both cases their orientation was political, even though their means may have differed. The next section examines how federal programs during this same period that were intended to improve inner-city school quality promoted other forms of citizen participation.

FEDERAL INITIATIVES TO IMPROVE INNER-CITY SCHOOLS

Compensatory Education

Even as desegregation riveted the nation's attention on the poor quality of inner-city schools, it provided have-nots of those cities opportunities to achieve educational equity through access to better resources and through oversight mechanisms that monitored the process. Yet the desegregation movement by itself did not focus on the need to improve the quality of the schools in poor neighborhoods. Separate federal programs were created to do this job, although later Northern desegregation orders required state funds for school improvement, as in Detroit and Chicago. Although the Emergency School Aid Act (ESAA) provided several hundred million dollars between 1972 and 1982 to facilitate desegregation programs, economically disadvantaged children, defined as those whose families were below the federal poverty line in income, received a much larger infusion of federal education funds with the passage of the Elementary and Secondary Education Act (ESEA) in 1965. These funds, which by 1981 were nearly $3.5 billion a year, were intended to supplement and improve the education of these children. Title I of ESEA was revised and is now known as Chapter I of the Educational Consolidation and Improvement Act (ECIA) of 1981.

Compensatory education refers to a broad spectrum of educational programs for disadvantaged students from infancy to adulthood. Funded principally with ECIA money ($3.5 billion per year), they are also funded by other federal acts passed between 1962 and 1972 (an additional $2 billion per year). Preschool programs range from infant education and intervention in family life to Head Start, which was the most prominent of all compensatory education programs. In 1984, Head Start served approximately 20 percent of children in poverty in that age bracket. Other programs focus on reading, language, and basic skills development; on bilingual education; or on guidance and counseling. There are programs to create new instructional materials, to prevent dropping out of school, to train teachers, and to add school personnel, such as teacher aides and paraprofessionals. There have been funds for tutoring programs, for reorganizing the school day, and for assistance to school personnel in dealing with desegregation problems. There are also special programs to assist disadvantaged students in higher education and adults who are illiterate or need training in basic skills (Ornstein & Levine, 1985).

Although earlier evaluations of compensatory education programs concluded that they produced little change, later investigations—after 1975—reported positive results. Ornstein and Levine suggest that compensatory education will not produce meaningful and permanent gains for most disadvantaged students, because they hold that schools exert only a "modest" influence on later achievement (1985, p. 417). However, it could also be argued that even though these compensatory education funds constitute almost 80 percent of

U.S. Department of Education funds, this expenditure is not nearly enough, given the scale of the problems. Chapter 3 alluded to the murky area of school finance whereby compensatory funds are used in place of local and state tax dollars instead of as a supplement to them. Minority leaders have long held this suspicion, but it has been difficult to verify through research. The discussion will now proceed to two other categories, one within compensatory education and one in addition to it, that led to the creation of citizen participation vehicles.

Multicultural Education

Awareness of the fallacy of the melting-pot ideal of American education began to grow during the 1950s and 1960s. There were and are many cultures represented within our schools, which created problems in language of instruction. Two opposing goals clashed: Should the schools educate for assimilation, stressing Standard English, or should they educate for self-esteem, emphasizing respect for one's different culture and language? Yet even when school officials and community might agree on one goal, such as Standard English, there is disagreement over how best to achieve it. Should limited-English-speaking (LES) or non-English-speaking (NES) students be taught in their native language over a long period of time, or should they be taught in English as soon as possible? Conflict and confusion over these bilingual education programs, begun in 1969 after the passage of the Bilingual Education Act of 1968 and spurred by the 1974 Supreme Court decision in *Lau v. Nichols*, which decided in favor of Chinese children who had been denied instruction in their own language in San Francisco, has not slowed federal expenditures for such programs. Congressional appropriations for bilingual instruction increased from $7.5 million in 1969 to $139.4 million in 1984.

Although scholars disagree over the effectiveness of bilingual education programs in terms of boosting minority achievement levels, the standard theme of "too little, too late" rings clear. By itself, bilingual education does not appear to be enough, though this is not to say that it does not focus attention on the important issue of school improvement for have-not children. Weinberg (1983) cites evidence that bilingual education has at best been minimally implemented, and that educators have often resisted court orders or have not been bilingual themselves. Where teachers are bilingual, they have shown positive attitudes toward bilingual instruction (p. 28). Given the propensity for school systems to discriminate against minority and low-income children, multicultural programs may function as a smoke screen for bad education or they may trivialize the curriculum. They could even lead to new forms of segregation (Ornstein & Levine, 1985, p. 430). Nevertheless, they have provided an avenue for minority parents and citizens to participate in the education of their children through a variety of advisory councils, to be discussed below.

Education for All Handicapped Children

An area of federal initiative in education that is generally outside of compensatory education but that has not only provided mechanisms for parent involvement but is largely the result of parental pressure is the area of programs for handicapped children. Lobbying and lawsuits by parents of handicapped children who were excluded from education led to the enactment of three major federal laws: the Rehabilitation Act of 1973, which outlawed discrimination against handicapped persons in any program or activity receiving federal money; PL (Public Law) 93–380 in 1974, which authorized increased funds to states for special education services and required due process to preserve handicapped students' rights; and the Education for All Handicapped Children Act of 1975, PL 94–142, which determined that free appropriate public education was the fundamental right of every handicapped person.

The total number of handicapped students receiving educational services under these acts between 1977 and 1983 increased from 3.7 to 4.3 million. Very large increases occurred in the categories of learning disabled and emotionally disturbed, while all other categories (for example, speech-, hearing-, visually-, or orthopedically impaired) declined in numbers. These two increasing categories contain disproportionate numbers of minority students, prompting critics to charge that this is how teachers suffering culture shock behave: Separate these students and get them out into special programs. Blacks are three times as likely as whites to be assessed "educable mentally retarded," while Native Americans are almost twice as likely to be so assessed (Ornstein & Levine, 1985).

It is not a surprise that urban school districts are where the learning disabled, the emotionally disturbed, and the educable mentally retarded students are concentrated. Thousands of these and other handicapped students are on waiting lists in urban centers because the federal mandates did not provide the funding needed to carry them out. Pressure by parents to create equitable laws was not enough to keep school systems from discriminatory labeling or to prod them to provide the funds to support adequate special programming.

Finally, mention should be made of a particular problem with its use as a tool of reform in urban schools. The categories mentioned above, learning disability, emotional disturbance, and educable mental retardation, are difficult to define; but even when adequate operational definitions have been generated, it is not clear how these handicaps should be addressed through schooling. There does not appear to be conclusive evidence whether restricted settings (where the handicapped are instructed in isolation from normal children—about 32 percent are in self-contained special classrooms or schools) or mainstreaming with normal children is the better way. Many educators feel that the less restricted the better as long as the child is learning. The main positive outcome of mainstreaming appears to be affective: the social acceptance of handicapped children by normal children.

In 1973, I was conducting a research project in a suburban school with a reputation for its commitment to open education. About two dozen of the 350 students were educable mentally retarded, with an assortment of physical handicaps as well. Although they spent most of their time in a separate classroom building, they were mainstreamed into many school activities, such as assemblies, films, or plays. I was impressed at how well the normal children accepted them, despite their obvious outward differences. Sadly, however, the one black child in the school, normal in every way, was the butt of many jeers and jokes. The staff had done a wonderful job in teaching the children tolerance only for different white children.

Citizen Advisory Councils Resulting from Federal Initiatives

Even as support for federal funding of local education agencies (LEAs) to provide increased services for poor children built toward passage of ESEA in 1965, acceptance of parent involvement as a necessary adjunct also grew. As early as 1964, then Secretary of Health, Education, and Welfare (HEW) Wilbur Cohen publicly approved the idea of participation by parents in federally funded child development programs (Summary of History of Title I, n.d.). The Kerner Commission Report of 1968 indicated that increased community and parental participation in the school system was basic to the successful function of the inner-city school. In 1966, PL 89-750 amended Title I to include a provision for community involvement, and in 1968, federal guidelines suggested that parent advisory councils be established for Title I by LEAs. By 1970, PL 91-230 gave the

Commissioner of Education discretion to regulate parent involvement for any education program for which he determined it was essential; a year and a half later he exercised that discretion by making district-wide parent advisory committees (PACs) and parent involvement for ESEA Title I a federal requirement. PL 93–380 in 1974 on behalf of handicapped students provided that PACs be required for each district and each school served by the program. Membership of these PACs was to be selected by parents; a majority must also be parents. In 1974 also, a national conference, endorsed by the U.S. Office of Education, was held in St. Louis, Missouri, to provide in-service training for parents. At this conference began the National Coalition of ESEA Title I Parents.

The federal model of the Title I PAC is the prototype of the citizen advisory council in education, but it was by no means the first type of citizen advisory council. That honor belongs to a citizen advisory council formed in Berkeley, California, in 1919 (Davies et al., 1979). Taking their cue from federal initiatives, some states, particularly California, Florida, and South Carolina, created PACs in all their districts in 1972 and 1973. These were to be more than mere PTAs; they were to advise—and only advise—on many heretofore sacrosanct school matters, including personnel, evaluation, budget, and curriculum. National foundations, particularly C. S. Mott and Rockefeller, have funded projects in support of citizen advisory councils in education.

Citizen advisory councils, despite their lack of actual political power, may be effective in certain cases in promoting school improvement. Where its role has been agreed upon by all constituents, where its membership is representative of the parent body, and where its resources are adequate to its task, the PAC has been able to achieve school improvement. There is evidence, however, that in most cases school administrators resisted low-income parent involvement in school policymaking, using these PACs instead as distant "early warning" systems for potential upset within the parent body. Three studies of Title I PACs agreed in their findings that the role of parents in education decision making was severely constrained, if not nonexistent (Weinberg, 1983).

One PAC, in Rochester, New York, did achieve early success in making educational changes, such as eliminating marginal school programs or initiating other programs. Its influence was due to its close connections with sophisticated community organizations. Its leaders were experienced in dealing with top administrators and possessed many connections with citywide sources of political influence. However, the central school administration reorganized the PAC after two years, replacing its leadership with much less sophisticated "grass-roots" representatives, and its influence declined rapidly thereafter.

Two other studies of the influence of school-community councils established under various grant programs verify the tendency of school officials to obstruct and coopt them. Where minority groups used governmental sources and outside support groups, as did Chicanos in Los Angeles in the early 1970s, they actually achieved incremental gains, such as some jobs for their members and new programs. Chicano leaders, though, tended to view Anglo willingness to accede to their demands as a political ploy to insert Chicanos as a buffer between Anglos and blacks.

In summary, parent advisory councils, even where there was disproportionate representation by middle-class parents, have tended to be dominated by principals, who set the agendas and decided what would be done with the councils' recommendations. School systems, having established these councils under federal or state mandate, too often have employed them as foils to allay public fears about the quality of their children's education rather than as channels for problem solving.

Before turning to the community control movement as a struggle for more than advisory power for citizens, we should mention child advocacy groups briefly to distinguish them from other citizen groups.

Child Advocacy Groups

These are not groups of parents or other have-not citizens, but coteries of highly sophisticated researchers and attorneys whose goal is to intervene either in individual cases or bring class actions where children's rights in education (or elsewhere) appear to be violated. These are not membership groups as are some parent bodies or neighborhood organizations, though they may solicit funds nationally, considering contributors as members. Child advocacy groups have been extraordinarily successful in promoting the rights of handicapped children and those in need of bilingual education. Usually they will press for legislation, and, having obtained it, will monitor it to see that its provisions are enforced.

BOTTOM-UP COMMUNITY CONTROL
AND DECENTRALIZATION OF SCHOOLS

Just as the drive for desegregation and the rapid increase in federal funding of programs for the education of the poor gave rise to diverse forms of citizen participation, both mandated and grassroots in origin, so also did the trends toward decentralization and community control of urban schools. This section examines three types of bottom-up community control: (1) focused inside public schools; (2) focused outside public schools; and (3) leading to system decentralization from the top down (Davies et al., 1979). In all cases the intent was to shift actual power in policymaking from the system to those previously dispossessed: parents and other community members, especially minorities and low-income persons.

Focused Inside Public Schools

The following four cases demonstrate reasonable success of community control focused inside the school.

Crystal City School System. An example of this first type of movement occurred in Crystal City, Texas. Since the period of Anglo invasion of the Southwest prior to the Civil War, the economic and political position of Mexican-Americans declined even as the larger economy of the area expanded (Weinberg, 1983). Public schools, previously willing to teach in the Spanish language, refused to do so after about 1850, even though Chicano enrollments soared. Schools currently reflect the cultural inequities that Anglo communities have heaped upon Chicanos. The mean achievement scores of Chicano students average two to three years behind their Anglo counterparts despite federal desegregation and bilingual initiatives. In general, Mexican-Americans suffer the same educational deprivation that other low-income minorities experience, a plight that derives, as we have seen, from larger patterns of economic and political discrimination in the community.

In Crystal City, Chicanos, who constituted more than 75 percent of the population, felt the same stirrings of ethnic consciousness that informed the black civil rights movement during the later 1950s and early 1960s. By 1965, they had elected five of their members to the city council, only to lose these seats in the subsequent election. By 1969, the battle lines were drawn, waiting for a mobilizing issue. It came in the form of discrimination against Chicanos as high-school cheerleaders; they were clearly underrepresented on the cheerleading squad. Student protest over this issue was supported by Jose Angel Guitierrez, a native of Crystal City and the founder of the Mexican American Youth Organization (MAYO) and later of the Raza Unida Party.

Student demands had a solid organizational base, but Guitierrez made it clear that the students were initiating action, not MAYO.

MAYO, more a civil rights group than a neighborhood organization, aimed at using the students' initiative to rekindle the enthusiasm of the parents. This combination of student leadership in school and political support in the community enabled the protest movement to keep the pressure on the school board to resolve their grievances. A student walkout and protest march led to a boycott by elementary students as well. Students had enlisted their parents' support and had received it. Subsequent organizing activity, which also brought in two mediators from the U.S. Department of Justice, led to the school board's giving in on nearly every demand.

Guitierrez's Raza Unida Party, organized in 1970, was to claim electoral control of both the city council and the school board within a year and a half. Bilingual programs were developed, and Chicano teachers became a majority on the faculty. Five students were made ex officio nonvoting members of the school board. Despite Anglo resistance, Chicano organizing brought the schools to reflect the cultural majority and to develop closer ties with the Chicano heritage.

This investigative account of the transition in the Crystal City school system does not mention the final relationship between the displaced Anglos, now a political as well as a numerical minority, and the Chicanos, now exerting much more political power. The tone of the report suggests that relations remain tense at best, even though Chicano students are better served and are becoming fluent in two languages, English and Spanish. Where organizing to gain power for have-nots succeeds, it must, if at all possible, seek to adjudicate the real needs of the minorities previously in control. In schools, these children deserve a good education, and they and their parents will serve better as allies than as hostile opposition forces. David Rogers and Norman Chung (1983) found that the dominance of one ethnic group over another, Puerto Ricans over Jews in one of New York's decentralized Community School Districts, led to prolonged conflict, which postponed constructive change in the schools. This wrangling need not be the only possible outcome of interethnic conflict, but leaders must try to advance beyond it.

Three other cases of successful community control within the public school system serve to reinforce the hypothesis that serious forms of community control within these systems will encounter furious resistance and will be under continuous threat to their existence. They are like genetic sports, so deviant from the norm of professional control as to become rapidly extinct.

Roosevelt Community School.   The Roosevelt Community School in Louisville, Kentucky, is the vestige of an attempt by the school superintendent to decentralize the entire system in the early 1970s (Davies, 1981). Located in a poor neighborhood, 80 percent white and 20 percent black, the school enjoyed strong neighborhood support and leadership by its principal, Car Foster. Three factors characterized this experiment. The first was a conscious attempt to make the school a center of community activity; parents were involved in tutoring and parent education programs, among others. Parent involvement was to lead to parent participation in decision making. The second factor in the experiment was that formal attention was paid to the real barriers between school professionals and parents. This moat was to be bridged by training and workshops for both parents and staff. The third factor was the structure of the community school board, which was composed of parents, other community residents, teachers, and other school staff, collaborating as equals. The board had broad powers to determine policy, interview and recommend personnel for hiring, evaluate these personnel, and set priorities for programs.

The Roosevelt Community School came under threat, however, as it entered the decade of the 1980s. The merger of the Louisville and Jefferson County school districts coupled with the loss of its principal followed upon the heels of two attempts by the central board to close the school.

Adams Morgan School.   The well-known Adams Morgan School Project in Washington, D.C., was a public elementary school experimentally turned over to community control in the spring of 1967 (Lantner, 1968). Its experimental nature included not only a community school board but also an innovative curriculum under the guidance of Antioch College. Much wrangling over control resulted in the closing of the school in 1974. The Adams Morgan School Project had received considerable sums of extra funding from the federal government and local foundations to hire community people. Apparently the parent advisory council spent too much time settling squabbles over who in the community would get the extra jobs to devote its energy to developing the school's educational program—a classic case of goal displacement.

BUILD Academy.   The BUILD Academy in Buffalo, New York (Brown, 1978), was the result of BUILD, an Alinsky organization that focused on the civil rights issues of the times: improvement in schools, desegregation, housing development, and employment programs. Its

issue with the school system was embodied in its demands for desegregation. While the organization was negotiating without success with the
Buffalo Board of Education about ending segregation in the schools, it
was called upon to intervene in a dispute between parents and school
officials at P.S. 32 in the center of the black community. The system had
dismissed a popular substitute teacher from the third-grade classroom to
make room for the return of a tenured teacher who had been on
maternity leave. Claiming insensitivity on the part of officials, and
supported by BUILD, parents and students boycotted the school, demanding the establishment of a community advisory board to make
policies for the school. The Buffalo School Board did create such a
board, which included twelve representatives from the neighborhood
and three each from the Buffalo Board of Education and the State
University College at Buffalo. However, the Buffalo Board of Education
retained veto power over the community advisory board.

Initially, major opposition came from the professional staff, who
perceived their jobs as threatened by this experiment. Nonetheless, the
school not only continued to function but also became a success in
terms of improved student achievement scores.

Several reasons have been given for this outcome:

1. The entire black community supported the concept.
2. The community school board experiment was conducted in
   one school only.
3. The Buffalo Board of Education took an active role in developing guidelines for the operation of the community school board.
4. The professional education associations did not formally oppose the experiment.
5. The superintendent and the Buffalo Board of Education retained final control of the experiment.
6. The community school board and the system never worked at
   cross purposes; that is, the decisions of the community school
   board never had to be overruled from above.
7. The community school board always sought the best teachers
   for the school.
8. The entire Buffalo community views the school as a success
   story.

In conclusion, astute and adroit political maneuvering that does not
threaten the power of the establishment, coupled with a climate amenable to change and a militant organizational base, will go far toward
ensuring success.

Focused Outside Public Schools

The second type of community control avoided the public school systems altogether. Whereas the first type was characterized by fierce power struggles for political power, the second was marked by struggles for economic survival. In all cases groups of parents and other community members tried to establish alternative school programs independent of the public school financial base. In some cases in the early 1970s, neighborhood organizations were the organizing base on which the school was built. In other situations the schools were already in existence as inner-city parochial schools about to be closed when parents and others, including the schools' staffs, cooperated to reopen them as separately incorporated community schools. Many other alternative schools were started on no preexisting foundation by a group of parents and other interested community residents.

The SAND Everywhere School. There are very few cases of multipurpose neighborhood organizations founding their own schools. One instance in which this occurred is instructive, however (Davies et al., 1979). The South Arsenal Neighborhood Development (SAND) organization in Hartford, Connecticut, established its own elementary school, the SAND Everywhere School, in the early 1970s. In 1975, however, it relinquished control to the public system. The result was the consolidation of the school from several buildings into one, the shift from an open-space concept to self-contained classrooms, and parents' loss of control over hiring of personnel.

Milwaukee's Federation of Independent Community Schools. Another type of school, built phoenix-like from a failing or defunct parochial school, is best exemplified by Milwaukee's Federation of Independent Community Schools. Eight inner-city elementary parochial schools were to be closed by the Archdiocese of Milwaukee for lack of funding. Parents, teachers (many of whom were religious sisters), black community leaders, and others, such as officials in Milwaukee's antipoverty programs and academics, understood that incorporating these schools as independent schools was but a tiny first step compared to securing a long-term financial base. Federal funds were available only for planning, not operations. United Community Services (United Fund), controlled by Protestant interests, did not fund educational programs. Foundation grants could not be relied upon for renewal. Low-income parents could not pay full tuition. Most of the schools held classes for a few years, but most were forced to close or reverted to parochial control.

Highland Community School.   I participated in the creation of yet another type of alternative school, joining with a young mother who was a Montessori teacher and two other women volunteers in 1969. We slowly created a small Montessori program, which we named the Highland Community School. Over time we added an elementary program to our preschool program, enrolling about sixty children between the ages of three and ten years, the majority of whom were low-income. Throughout the process our main interest was not only the quality of the children's education but also the control and ownership of the school by the parents of these children. From the beginning, the governing board was composed of five parents and only two staff members. The Highland Community School survives to this day, not only because of its manageable size and teachers' willingness to take very low pay, but also because its parents have carried it with their wise decisions and hard work. The school has also had an active advisory group of "first citizens" who have helped it attain resources and standing in the broader Milwaukee area.

Most alternative nonpublic schools not subsidized by a church have closed their doors, because they failed to develop a successful funding strategy to offset the low-income parents' inability to pay the full costs of schooling. Diane Ravitch (1983) estimated that fewer than 20,000 students attended the peak number of perhaps 500 "free schools" existing during the late 1960s and early 1970s. In addition, most of these children were probably not low-income but rather offspring of middle-income whites alienated from the public schools. The number of low-income minority students attending alternative schools created by their parents and supportive educators was considerably smaller, because their ability to pay the financial costs was proportionately lower.

In summary, the bottom-up, outside-the-system strategy of community control in education during this period was an effort doomed to failure in the heavily unequal struggle for resources with the giant public systems. That it had some successes is testimony to the disaffection of many parents with the public school system and to the depth of concern these people had for their children's education.

Leading to Top-Down Decentralization

New York City Public Schools.   The third strategy for community control, bottom-up leading to public school system decentralization from the top down, is best exemplified by the famous New York City experiment in community control that resulted in the creation of 32 districts under the direction of elected Community School Boards (CSBs). The community control experiments took place in three demonstration districts, each with several schools. When the CSB in the Ocean Hill-Brownsville district collided with the teachers' union (United Federation of Teachers) over firing and transfer policy, the union first struck the district, then the entire system, bringing a quick end to a separatist form of community control by 1970 (Havighurst, 1979).

The residue of this struggle between parents and system, however, was the decentralization of the nation's largest system into 32 districts each with a population the size of a medium-sized city (200,000 to 300,000). The powers of the CSBs that governed them were more circumscribed than under the original community control experiment. The CSBs could hire the district superintendent and later could fire principals as well, but they could only function in an advisory capacity on budget and curriculum matters (Davies et al., 1979).

A thorough study of the decentralization of New York's public school system indicates that more localized control has produced benefits, although critics think they are minimal at best (Rogers & Chung, 1983). Yet in spite of ethnic wars and other shortcomings in the beginning, there are signs of hope. Where there have been established parent and community organizations in operation (not political clubs, churches, or antipoverty agencies, however), there has tended to be an atmosphere of political stability in the CSB. These cohesive CSBs have assumed a policy role and have delegated administrative authority effectively, especially when they have worked with strong leaders as district superintendents. Student achievement scores in these districts are up and vandalism is down. Such decentralization may also have helped stem the tide of white flight from successful districts. The New York City schools have gained some legitimacy since the 1960s in minority neighborhoods. And the district superintendents and principals have a new orientation toward the community rather than to the system, enabling them to develop new linkages and programs.

248095

Detroit Public Schools. The second major experiment in school system decentralization took place in the Detroit public schools after Coleman Young, then a state senator, submitted a plan to create eight regional districts with elected boards under one central board. His plan arose out of controversy not only about the quality of Detroit's schools but also about desegregation. Although the plan was implemented, confusion over goals and the decision in *Milliken v. Bradley*, which refused to extend busing for desegregation into neighboring suburbs, combined to minimize the effectiveness of this thrust to promote greater citizen control of local schools. Detroit's future appears to hold recentralization of its public school system.

The New York and Detroit cases represent a drive for political control of schools by have-nots. The Los Angeles call for decentralization was not primarily political but rather organizational in tone. Although there had been established such alternative schools as the Malcolm X Montessori School and the Westminster Neighborhood Association School, the plan to decentralize the system was an administrative strategem to involve principals as key agents in community relations (O'Shea, 1975). Its purpose was to decrease the potential for community conflict against the system rather than to increase citizen participation in educational decision making.

SUMMARY

The drive for citizens to control their inner-city schools saw three outcomes during the decade spanning the mid-1960s to the mid-1970s. Where parents and other community members sought significant political control over public schools, they encountered resistance from several quarters, both within and outside the system. They were most likely to be successful if they focused their energies on only one school. Establishment of control over a subdistrict or complex of schools, as in the New York experiment, showed mixed results. The second demand for control found form in the creation of alternative schools outside the system. These new schools struggled for economic survival from the outset, and most of them closed permanently or were absorbed into the public system. The third outcome of political agitation to improve have-nots' schools was the creation of decentralization schemes, only two of which—in New York and Detroit—actually began to devolve power or share it more widely with citizens. Although decentralization of the large urban systems may allow a relatively few more citizens into the decision-making process, it may pave the way for citizens to gain influence more easily in the particular school their children attend.

The purpose of these last two chapters has been to highlight examples and categories of citizen participation in the operation of schools that serve their communities. These communities, however, have undergone discontinuous changes. Cities came to dominate the economy; agrarian folkways gave way to urban lifestyles; social organization declined in the face of social disorganization. Discrepancies between wealth and poverty, exaggerated in this country compared with other industrialized nations at present, have produced a poverty population nearing 50 million persons, disproportionately minority and urban.[2]

One child in five lives in poverty. The schools these urban children attend show the marks of a century of bureaucratization, though the rigidity of the first bureaucracies controlling them has softened as other forces gained policy power. Teachers unions, the federal government, colleges of education, rebellious taxpayers, and courts have all effectively applied pressure to schools. There is a long history of parents and other citizens attempting to gain footholds on the policymaking process, but they have not made a breach in school establishment walls to the same extent that more institutionalized forces have. Have-not citizens especially have not found a widely accepted manner of institutionalizing themselves as an interest bloc in the operation of their public schools. Low-income citizens have used litigation, boycotts, and even violence trying to gain meaningful entry to local school policymaking, but they have rarely succeeded in forcing lasting changes on their schools.

The neighborhood organization movement of the past two decades represents the appearance of a form of citizen participation on a wide basis that lends itself to helping low-income citizens gain access to school policymaking on behalf of their children. The next chapter investigates the rise of neighborhood organizations and examines where they have attempted to lower the drawbridge over the moat between school and low-income neighborhood.

7

Multi-Issue Neighborhood Organizations

The urban crisis meant my block. (Cincotta, 1986)

Ineffective instruction is the result of organizational maladaptation by schools to low-income students. It is rooted in the structural relations between haves and have-nots in American society. This relation underlies the ignorance with which urban schools approach their job and the unavailability of human and financial resources when they do try to approach the task in an enlightened way. Many poor communities have not organized themselves to overcome these disadvantages, but the widespread appearance of local community organizations in low-income neighborhoods in recent years signals the possibility that parents could employ them as vehicles for urban school reform.

Collective citizen action as a means of change for relatively powerless people is as old in American cities as the cities themselves. Yet the forms it has taken have evolved over the decades, retaining vestiges of the old while devising anew. The previous chapter chronicled federal initiatives in education that gave impetus to citizen participation; other federal programs to aid the poor also gave sustenance to popular activism already in place, such as the civil rights movement and the organizations founded by Saul Alinsky and his students.

This chapter, in an attempt to define the phenomenon of contemporary neighborhood organizations, prefaces a list of its general characteristics with a discussion of federal initiatives that have influenced them. It then looks more specifically at variables essential to the functioning organization, namely, leadership, motivation, goals, issues, norms, and group evolution. The chapter closes by first examining them as mediating institutions and then comparing neighborhood organizations with single-issue parents' groups as to their potential effectiveness in reforming urban schools.

THE INFLUENCE OF FEDERAL INITIATIVES

The Economic Opportunity Act of 1964, with its call for "the maximum feasible participation of residents of the areas and members of the groups to be served," was the first formal recognition of the need to include the voices of the poor in planning for their "reclamation" (James, 1973, p. 183). Municipal interests, represented by the League of Cities and Conference of Mayors, lobbied successfully, however, to ensure that poor persons would not gain access to positions of power in the War on Poverty's Community Action Programs. Model Cities legislation in 1966, therefore, deliberately vested control of poverty funds in City Hall. In 1974, though, the Community Development Block Grant (CDBG) program, which replaced Model Cities, brought new potential for citizen involvement in planning distribution of funds for community redevelopment. In many of the 3,000 municipalities to obtain CDBG funds since then, citizens have carved out a place for themselves in advising on their allocation. Some CDBG funds have even supported neighborhood organizing. The impact of the Reagan New Federalism approach, which would let state governments dole out funds to municipalities, according to one observer, would be to reduce these funds, scatter them, and make them less effective (Kettl, 1981).

Other federal programs have had an effect on citizen participation in the neighborhood movement. Volunteers in Service to America (popularly known as VISTAs) acted as neighborhood organizers in some cases during the 1960s and 1970s, as did CETA (Comprehensive Employment and Training Act) and Neighborhood Youth Corps workers. Congress, prodded by neighborhood groups from Chicago and elsewhere, passed several pieces of banking legislation between 1975 and 1980 that enabled neighborhood organizations to monitor lending practices and to push successfully for $3 billion in loans for housing development in low-income areas. Each of these instruments reinforced the citizen involvement movement.

Today's neighborhood organization in economically depressed areas has its origins not only in these federal acts and the Alinsky tradition but also in a new populism that followed the roily 1960s. This vague ideological mutation was wary of professionals and hostile to bureaucracy, as it had always been, but it appeared less idealistic and more rooted in the practical concerns and social fabric of the neighborhood. Local problems, not great social issues, were its agenda.

Yet this latest cultural twist is not a reversal of 1960s idealism. Folded into its emphasis on self-interest and turf consciousness is a large portion of social sophistication about the evils of institutional control, an awareness that one's small struggle against local institutional bullies is part of a larger scheme, although this acknowledgment may often be imprecise or wrongheaded. It is steeped in a new national consciousness, rooted in the Vietnam experience and subsequent economic decline, that America may not be pure, that it may be just like other powerful nations, doing what it deems it must to protect its foreign interests and maintain status quo at home, no matter what the cost in money, lives, unemployment, or poverty. Mistrust of big business parallels this emergence from social naïveté.

Neighborhood organizations, flourishing in cities everywhere, embody this populism. Their potential use for school reform on behalf of victims of poverty is the subject of the remainder of this book.

CHARACTERISTICS

People getting together to solve a problem they all face is as old a tactic as the human race. Organizing currently carries a much narrower meaning, however; it signifies initiating collective action by relatively poor or powerless people to solve their common problems. The first chapter demonstrated that the sources of these problems are complex, invisibly woven into bureaucracies and difficult to attack. So organizing begins by clarifying the problem so that people can begin to take a hand in solving it. But organizers not only clarify, they also define the problem so that its solution is advantageous to these people. Neighborhood organizing deals with public problems common to residents of a particular neighborhood or several neighborhoods.

Neighborhood organizations are a particular form of citizen-initiated action group. They share the political orientation of public interest research groups (such as Ralph Nader's Public Citizen), the issues of civil rights groups, the democratic openness of self-help groups (Alcoholics Anonymous, for example), the pride of place of a chamber of commerce, and the social networking of a parish, a labor union, or a community center. But they are none of these.

Following is a description of the general characteristics of neighborhood organizations (Williams, 1985).

1. The urban neighborhood organization is geographically localized and draws its strength from the residents' "identification with the turf." This characteristic is central in importance. It implies geographic borders, a mild sense of threat to the neighborhood, a sense

of satisfaction in living there—even if by objective standards it is deteriorating badly. Among its leaders there is a sense of commitment to the neighborhood that goes beyond mere satisfaction with living there.

2. The neighborhood organization is a citizen-initiated action group that seeks greater voice in decisions that affect the neighborhood.

3. Its internal structure is intended to be democratic; that is, it allows accountability to its members and its membership is open to all residents.

4. It avoids overt allegiance to particular political ideologies, but it tends to be populist and reformist in its perspective. There are, however, many historical examples, especially in white ethnic, middle-class neighborhoods, of very reactionary groups.

5. It usually operates in older, economically depressed areas, although there is considerable activity in middle-class areas as well.

6. Its organizational size and structure tend to fit its goals for neighborhood improvement and the resources available to it. For example, the big-city federations are structured to combat problems of a big-city scale. Their budgets and staffs are proportionately larger.

7. It addresses several issues simultaneously in order to maintain a broad base of support. It may persist over a long period, however, while it focuses on only one major issue, such as housing or police-community relations.

8. It uses a variety of strategies to achieve its ends. Chief among these are
   • putting demands on institutions,
   • using conventional electoral politics, and
   • developing alternative economic or service institutions.

9. Most neighborhood organizations do not employ a staff. If these organizations exist in low-income areas for some time, however, they are highly likely to employ organizers at least. The sources of their funding range from individual resident contributions to church, foundation, or government grants.

Successful neighborhood organizations share several traits (Perlman, 1976). Among these are paid staff, clear goals, well-developed fund-raising capacity, and a sophisticated mode of operation. This last characteristic includes effective street organizing and issue-research capabilities, information dissemination and exposé techniques, lobbying, confrontation and negotiation skills, good management capability in service delivery or economic development projects, policy and planning capacity, and experience in monitoring and evaluating government programs and grants. Success also requires a broadening viewpoint, which sociologist Janice Perlman labeled "issue growth from neighborhood to nation" (1976, p. 20), access to support networks that provide appropriate training and technical assistance, and coalition building with other such groups and supportive third parties, such as unions or public interest research groups.

Failed or unsuccessful neighborhood organizations were deficient in one or more of these traits. They became isolated from prevailing social movements or lost sight of their constituency; their internal structure was unable to resolve the inevitable disputes between members; they made few appeals to third parties; their issue selection was poor; and as a result, they experienced funding difficulties (Lancourt, 1979).

LEADERSHIP

Leadership in neighborhood organizations is the element most essential to their effective functioning. Leaders, in general, whether officially chosen or emergent, tend to take the initiative in analyzing situations and acting upon this analysis, but they must also remain flexible in the face of follower response. Leadership research suggests that leader styles of interaction, such as authoritarian, democratic, or laissez-faire, are dependent upon the context. Few people are capable of exerting all styles equally well, which leads to the conclusion that in a neighborhood organization several people at least will fill leadership roles as contexts change.

Urban leaders are of several kinds (Nix, 1976, pp. 313-24): legitimizers, effectors, activists, and the general public. Legitimizers are policymakers in the public and private sectors, those whose authority rests on their position, such as mayors, police chiefs, or bank presidents. Effectors are the managers in large institutions, professionally trained bureaucrats whose power flows from their technical knowledge and ability to manipulate financial and material resources. These first two types exert the lion's share of influence in a city.

At a much lower level of influence are the third and fourth types of urban leader. Activists are doers and joiners, but they lack technical skills and a power base. The general public contains many who exert a passive leadership through their voting patterns and influence on immediate peers at work or in the neighborhood. The neighborhood organization leadership is usually drawn from these latter two types.

Neighborhood

Curt Lamb's (1975) study of leadership in poor neighborhoods in 100 American cities produced five clusters of neighborhood leader types. Interviews with 8,000 residents in these poverty areas asked these individuals to name one or more leaders in their neighborhood exclusive of heads of institutions or large organizations. The resulting 630 leaders so identified clustered into five types: neighborhood radicals, respectable militants, the uninvolved, the elder elite, and the neighborhood establishment.

Thirty-three percent of these leaders were neighborhood radicals who belonged to citizen action groups such as tenant, welfare, or civil rights organizations. They were intensely angry at their neighborhood conditions, were alienated from local and national government, and avoided traditional groups, such as PTAs and other civic or professional groups. Another 20 percent Lamb characterized as respectable militants, who though active in protest, differed from the first group of radicals in belonging to traditional groups and in being far less hostile toward government. A third group constituting 9 percent of the sample was labeled the uninvolved. Though not politically active at the moment, they indicated they were on the verge of greater involvement.

These three categories represent a leadership pool most likely to spearhead neighborhood organizing for social change, with the radicals the most potent of the three. Lamb's remaining two categories complicate the picture, however. The second largest category at 27 percent were the elder elite. Older than the others and lower in income and education, these persons represented the end result of the exodus of the most effective leaders from the local area. Although they were cynical about local government, they retained little influence as their civic involvement diminished. They were unlikely to be activists or leaders in the neighborhood organizations.

The last group, encompassing the final 11 percent of the total, was the neighborhood establishment. Even though they were below the norm in education, they were the highest of all in income and tended to be conservative in their view of local problems, particularly in seeing poverty as the result of personal inadequacy. They were not angry, because their perception of community problems was superficial, but they exerted extraordinary influence through their regular contact with influential officials. They formed a leadership pool capable of obstructing the progressive neighborhood organization as it pressed its agenda for change. Robert Bailey (1972) reported on just such a clash in his study of the formation of the Organization for a Better Austin (OBA) in the Chicago area.

Lamb's extensive study discovered that leaders in poor neighborhoods are authentic representatives of the residents at large; they are long-term residents themselves with slightly higher levels of income and education than their neighbors. Their neighborhoods are experiencing serious economic and social problems that are not being effectively addressed by local politicians. Consequently, residents feel powerless to change neighborhood conditions and harbor a degree of alienation from government, which is magnified in their leadership, with the exception of the neighborhood establishment. Nonetheless, these leaders are oriented toward social participation. Their personal resources (education, interpersonal skills, and stamina—to attend up to 200 meetings a year) and their history of grassroots involvement are greater than those of their neighbors. This fact does not deny the influence of so-called outside professional organizers, hired to create and run big-city coalitions of organizations. But without a pool of these resident leaders, no organizing will retain long-term staying power. Their motives are a combination of altruistic commitment to the neighborhood's rehabilitation, self-interest, as in the case of parents' interest in their children's education, and simple social needs to belong, to contribute to community, or to gain esteem among peers (Rich, 1980; Ballenger, 1981). These leaders are also committed to improving their neighborhood, not being satisfied merely with residing there (Ahlbrandt & Cunningham, 1979). Their commitment is grounded in identification with the place.

The neighborhood organizer is also a leader, but a special one. In the Alinsky-style federations of local organizations that have operated mostly in big cities since before World War II, organizers have become highly trained professionals, paid in the $20,000 to $40,000 salary range, who function somewhat as advisors or consultants to the group (Leff, 1981). Trained at the Industrial Areas Foundation, these individuals will not go into an area unless invited by a "sponsoring committee," a group of local and regional church leaders who wish to see the organizing process take root through the local churches (Organizing, 1978). They must raise a two-year supply of money to support the organizers before they can retain their services. The objective is to build a large organization, representative of the residents, that can begin to exert leverage on the major issues of interest to them.

In urban areas other than the great cities, neighborhood organizations, if they employ organizers, are more likely to hire local residents who are less trained, if indeed they have any training at all. Organizers exist across a spectrum of ability and experience, mediated by some two dozen training centers in the U.S. Most have come from the ranks of local neighborhood leaders, and share their characteristics with the one exception that they are paid—though meagerly in most cases—for their efforts.

GOALS, STRUCTURE, ISSUES, AND NORMS

Joan Lancourt (1979), a former Alinsky organizer, studied the successes and failures of eight Alinsky organizations. In doing so, she developed a typology of organizational goals that is applicable to most neighborhood organizations. The primary goal was to create an organization accountable to the residents, since none of the politicians or other legitimizers or effectors seemed to be. Other long-range goals included stabilizing the community (preventing further decline), encouraging resident participation, promoting social justice, and disseminating necessary information to the residents. These goals might conflict with one another, however, as in the case where stabilizing the community may be conceived as driving out or keeping out a class of have-nots, which frustrates the goal of social justice. Intermediate-range goals were development of organizational capacity, acquisition of organizational power, and neighborhood control of neighborhood resources. The one short-term but difficult goal was victory in the campaigns the organization waged. These campaigns were formed on specific issues, to be discussed below.

The structure of the organization usually includes an elected or representative board of residents, which sets organizational policy and directs staff. In the smaller neighborhood organizations, the board actually operates more as a group of volunteers who work with the organizer. In larger community organizations, such as federations or coalitions, the board is a group of representatives elected or appointed by the staffs or constituencies of their respective organizations. In these larger organizations, the board monitors yearly organizing priorities set at the annual congress, a convention of several hundred delegates from the member organizations. Staff organizers in all cases are hired to promote ceaselessly participation through research and information dissemination, to call meetings of interested residents, and to consult on problem definition and the devising of tactics, monitoring of outcomes, and providing feedback to residents.

Opinions on the issues differ about bad neighborhood conditions precisely in the way that they are defined as problems. Since the definition of a problem implies its solution, the neighborhood organization always seeks to define the neighborhood's common problems to the advantage of the neighborhood. An example of this process occurred at the beginning of The Woodlawn Organization (TWO) in a black ghetto just south of the University of Chicago. The housing on the border between the two, occupied by low-income blacks, had deteriorated badly. The university defined the problem to its advantage: raze the buildings to make room for new student housing. The residents' organization defined the problem to *their* advantage: this is our housing, and the university and the city should help us rehabilitate or replace it for our people.

Issues of multipurpose neighborhood organizations harbor unique qualities (Alinsky, 1972b). Not only are issues created out of bad conditions, they are also controversial. They must be multiple in order to meet the different priorities of the members, and they must be "specific, immediate, and realizable" (Alinsky, 1972b, p. 119). Typically these issues have focused on crime and public safety, housing rehabilitation (ranging from improvement to code enforcement clampdowns on landlords), economic development (often through special spin-off agencies called community development corporations), recreation, public infrastructure maintenance and improvement (streets, curbs, parks, traffic patterning), energy (particularly weatherization and dissemination of conservation information), and education.

If *issues* are the lifeblood of a neighborhood organization, its norms of operation are the unseen bones that support the entire structural mass of the organization. *Norms* are the standards or rules that govern the behavior of the organization's leaders and members. They may be formal or informal, conscious or unconscious (many of the most important operational norms are unspoken). Most norms are similar to those of other organizations, often quite different in purpose, such as norms for conducting meetings, publication of information, and internal communication.

A group that conducts confrontational campaigns requires special dos and don'ts, not only for the conflict itself, but also to avoid the pitfalls that productive leaders and organizers must avoid. Saul Alinsky wrote aphorisms for effective militant collective action that have stood the test of time (1972b, pp. 127–31). For example, "A good tactic is one that your people enjoy" or "Make the enemy live up to their book of rules" are among dozens that he coined. Other norms to circumvent burnout in the neighborhood organization leadership are the need for clear direction in the work environment; to say no to escalating demands on one's time; to provide rewards, especially adequate salary, to organizers; to achieve some success (victory); and to provide a supportive network of friends and associates (Bryan, 1981). The successful organization is able to examine even its informal or unconscious norms to revise them where they lead to counterproductive behavior.

In summary, neighborhood organizations represent geographically localized citizen action groups, self-initiated rather than government mandated for the purpose of restoring accountability to local residents. These groups seek not only to be accountable themselves, but also to make institutions that affect the neighborhood accountable in ways they have not been heretofore. They have done this particularly well with respect to their elected representatives in City Hall because, despite the bureaucratic obstacles to communication with public officials, they do have access to them as voting citizens and taxpayers. They have somewhat less access to private corporations; what access they do have is through the regulatory powers of government and, in some cases, as employees or consumers. Schools, however, are theoretically the most accessible institutions of the neighborhood, since they are local and they interact a great deal with the neighborhood's children. Yet urban school systems have for the most part evaded or resisted have-not demands for accountability.

THE NEIGHBORHOOD ORGANIZATION AS MEDIATING INSTITUTION

A mediating institution is a group structure that stands between the private life of the individual and the giant megastructures of modern society, such as government, corporations, and other bureaucracies (Berger & Neuhaus, 1977). Examples are the family, the church, the school, the neighborhood, and the voluntary or civic association. "Standing between" implies a dual role: advocacy for the needs of the individual and education of the individual in coping with the outside world (Williams, 1985, pp. 223–25). Thus the mediating institution is both instrument and instructor; through the mediating institution, the person both acts and learns. Each role involves a fundamental tension in the case of the neighborhood organization. As advocate for its neighborhood, it makes demands on the megastructures that influence the area to recapture, retain, or improve scarce goods and services. Such actions create strained relations with these outside agencies. As internal educator, the neighborhood organization must attempt to unify diverse interests within the neighborhood, to bring residents together psychologically as well as physically through internal communication.

The neighborhood organization educates its membership in several ways. First, as Alinsky never ceased pointing out, the very process of acting collectively to redress their grievances educates those involved. For Alinsky, this was "popular education"; but those who are actively participating at any one time are a small fraction of the neighborhood population. Therefore, the neighborhood organization must educate in other ways. A second common mode of instruction is the neighborhood newsletter, which informs the residents on the progress of issue resolution. Block meetings are a third way that organizers and leaders can educate the populace. In some cases neighborhood organizations have functioned as adjudicators of disputes between neighbors; six San Francisco neighborhoods received formal foundation support to develop a program to settle minor grievances among residents (Fogarino, 1981). Finally, leaders can act as disciplinarians, teaching social responsibility to residents when appropriate. In viable neighborhoods this function is taken for granted: "If my kid makes too much noise or otherwise disturbs the peace, Mr. Grinstad or Mrs. Johnson will not hesitate to tell him to stop."

It is as the instrument of advocacy for the oppressed that the neighborhood organization generates reaction from the agencies that shape the neighborhood. The process of have-not citizens advocating on their own behalf is at bottom a management of perpetual conflict with haves (Williams, 1985). This conflict requires some explanation.

Conflict between two groups or organizations involves several factors (Katz & Kahn, 1978, pp. 618–20).

1. Some organizations are more likely to engage in conflict than others because they have units specialized to do so (army) or an ideology of conflict (union). Neighborhood organizations in low-income areas led by leaders alienated from government or the school system are very likely to carry an ethos of conflict.
2. Conflict arises out of a clash of interests; that is, the good of one side precludes that of the other. This conflict of interests may be real or only subjectively perceived by the parties. In addition, each side must be able to interfere in the operations of the other, which implies some degree of interdependence. Schools, of course, make no sense without the willing cooperation of the pupils and their parents.
3. The conflict between organizations is conducted by relatively small numbers of people in certain "boundary" positions. The behaviors

of these people are set by the role expectations of the respective memberships. In the neighborhood organizations, these boundary persons are the leaders, including, on some occasions, the organizers. Usually, however, though organizers may plan the action, the ideology of citizen participation requires that others enact it.

4. Personality and predisposition of each boundary person play a part in the neighborhood organization. Aggressive traits and hostile behavior in leaders are tolerated by their constituents, although they must manage these tendencies appropriately.

5. Norms, rules, and procedures represent constraints outside the organizations themselves that influence their conflict behavior. Neighborhood organizations operate within legal boundaries and do not advocate violence. They may engage in outrageous or embarrassing tactics, however, depending on their degree of alienation from the institution confronted.

Perhaps most important of all is the interaction of all these variables, that is, the actual behavior of those conducting the conflict. Once into the fray, the very process has its own dynamic of action and reaction. Escalation, or increasing the pressure until one side backs down, is a typical form of this dynamic. Escalation almost always works to the neighborhood organization's disadvantage because it closes off communication, shifts attention from what one's own group is gaining to what the other side is losing, spreads the conflict to other issues, and tends to break the relationship completely. In addition, the institution confronted is often in a far better position to withstand siege because of its superior resources. The effective neighborhood organization manages conflict by thinking in terms not only of what it can win but also of what the confronted institution can gain.

NEIGHBORHOOD ORGANIZATIONS AS VEHICLES FOR SCHOOL REFORM

The previous elaborated definition of the multipurpose neighborhood organization was necessary to buttress the argument that these groups are more effective vehicles for school reform than are single-issue parents' groups (Davies et al., 1979). Here are three reasons.

First, their superiority flows from their concern with all local matters directly affecting the neighborhood. Just as schools are meant to socialize youth, so also are neighborhood organizations builders of the social fabric. They will be concerned if, in fact, the local school is not only failing to socialize youth but at the same time functioning as a center for crime and vandalism. Both organizations, in other words, have as a major purpose the social control of the neighborhood. If one is not doing its job here, the other will demand that it do so. The school is also a local major institution affecting the neighborhood, just the sort to attract the attention of the local neighborhood organization. In addition, the parents and other residents want the same quality education afforded more affluent children. They care about what the school does, for their own children as well as for others. It is an issue for them, just as much as housing or crime.

This concern for addressing many types of problems in the neighborhood underlies the second reason why neighborhood organizations are better for dealing with schools: In their democratic openness they seek the broadest representation possible from the neighborhood. Although this ideal may not always be reached, holding it as a goal ensures that a broad constituency will be built to underwrite the long-term existence of the organization. Promoting reform is a long-term proposition, especially in schools. Parent groups alone, especially elementary school parents, represent a much smaller base of support, and when their children leave the school, they often lose interest. The high mobility of low-income parents from neighborhood to neighborhood within the inner city further erodes this already small base.

The third reason is that a neighborhood organization is much more likely to employ a staff organizer to devote considerable time to organizing than is the local group solely interested in education. As noted earlier, research on neighborhood organization effectiveness seems to indicate that paid staff are a primary factor in achieving the organization's goals. But can low-income groups find the funds to pay organizers?

Low-income groups have succeeded in raising money from outside sources. Alinsky organizers now require a two- to three-year cushion of financial support (perhaps $250,000) from communities that seek their skills. This support usually comes from inner-city church groups organized into an umbrella coalition. Other large, mature organizations have received United Fund support (such as SECO in Baltimore—$150,000). Many cities have utilized various federal grant programs, most recently CDBG, to fund crime prevention or housing organizers in neighborhood organizations.

These groups have succeeded in raising money from their own residents as well, though the amounts raised are disproportionately small compared to the energy invested by the organizations' leaders.

Fund-raising potential, especially from its constituents, is basic to an advocacy organization's capability of employing organizers. This funding base exists for the neighborhood organization because it accomplishes three goals:

1. It can deliver services, ranging from the neighborhood newsletter, crime prevention, and housing referral, to day care, home maintenance, or economic development.
2. It can mobilize citizens on a variety of concrete issues, particularly as its track record grows.
3. It can build federations of local parishes, businesses, service organizations, and social service agencies, all of which have their own constituencies with fund-raising potential.

Fund-raising for a group devoted solely to education is much more problematic because of its smaller member base, single-issue focus, and difficulty in producing tangible results (such as improved reading scores).

Most neighborhood organizations, however, have not dealt with educational issues. They have built their track record on more immediate and tangible problems, such as housing deterioration, crime, public improvements, service delivery, or recreation. Many have focused primarily on economic development (Mayer, 1984). In addition, they may not have known how to deal with the problem of effective schooling, although this obstacle is a result of another, a lack of involvement in the organization by many parents of children in local elementary or secondary schools. There certainly have been cases where low-income groups have had clarity about what to demand from educators, but their organization did not develop enough political clout to carry it through.

I have argued thus far that neighborhood organizations, with their multiple-issue, advocacy focus, their concrete record of accomplishment, and their paid staff and constituency-based fund-raising potential, are better vehicles for launching organizing campaigns to improve urban schools than are single-issue parent groups. The next chapters will examine the meanings of parent and citizen involvement in schools; review cases of both success and failure in organizing for reform; and analyze factors most important in working toward improvement.

8

Exploring Organizational Linkages Between Neighborhood and School

Political activity begins with demands . . . The consumer of public educational services is responsible for deciding and making clear that he is demanding either more of the same or change. (Summerfield, 1971, p. 103)

This book is about collective interaction with and demands on schools by parents and other neighborhood residents. Most of the literature on parent or citizen involvement in education has either defined ways individual parents could become involved or outlined the effects of this individual involvement. Samples of this work begin this chapter. Its greater portion, however, studies theoretical forms of linkage whereby neighborhood people can interact collectively with the school. The work of Eugene Litwak and Henry Meyer (1974) has been especially helpful. The chapter will close with an evaluation of their theory.

MEANINGS OF PARENT/CITIZEN INVOLVEMENT IN EDUCATION

One observer, Eugenia Berger (1981, p. 95), listed six general categories of parental roles with respect to their children's school: that of spectator, teachers of their own children, "accessory volunteers," educational volunteers, employees, and policy makers. The most universal role is that of spectator, in which the parents view the school as an authority figure best able to handle the education of their children. Parents, of course, are also teachers of their own children, a role only recently acknowledged formally by the education establishment. A third role is that of parents as "accessory volunteers," in which the parent provides services unrelated to the educational process. Berger states this is the role of the "room-parent, who provides treats and creates parties" (p. 95). In schools for low-income children, particularly nonpublic schools, the accessory volunteer may do everything from fixing plumbing to working on fund-raisers. Parents function also as educational volunteers, performing tasks directly related to instruction. They may even be employees of the school's instructional or noninstructional staff. Finally they may act as policymakers. Berger's classification, however, suffers both from an emphasis on how parents can link with school on an individual basis and from a focus on parents alone as those nonprofessionals who should somehow be involved with the school.

Boston's Institute for Responsive Education, a research group devoted to the issue of citizen participation in education, has published a number of works on the matter of its definition. Don Davies, Director of the Institute, reduced the question to its subparts: the who, what, and why of citizen participation in education (1981, pp. 83–119).

Davies asked, who are the citizens who will participate? "Citizens" include parents or guardians, neighborhood residents, students or youth out of school, employees of the system, people in various "community interest" positions such as social service agencies, business, public safety, or neighborhood organization leaders, and finally, taxpayers or voters.

He then wanted to know, what are the functions served by participation? That is, what does participation mean? Davies listed six functions: authorizing, enabling, planning, governing, service-giving, and evaluating. *Authorizing* means legitimating policy approved by officials. An example might be a citizens' committee appointed by the school board to help convince the community to vote positively on a millage request. *Enabling* implies that the citizens help the school system acquire resources necessary for its work. An example in my experience is the local public elementary school asking parents to request from the central office a high playground fence after a car had driven across the open field while children were at play there. The fence was constructed after several parents spoke at a board meeting. *Planning* suggests that the citizens are somehow included in the creation of plans for new schools, closing of old ones, or changes in existing ones. For example, says Davies, a neighborhood group might do a needs-assessment survey for a proposed after-school program.

Governing indicates that citizens share power in personnel, budgeting, curriculum, and facilities decisions. This is not the same as community control. The Yale Child Study Center's King-Baldwin School Project, mentioned in Chapter 4, provides an example of a cooperative sharing of decision-making power between school and neighborhood. *Service-giving* refers to provision of direct services by citizens, such as parents tutoring students or volunteering to work in the library. *Evaluating* includes monitoring of programs by citizens and making judgments about their effectiveness. Parents, for example, might be involved in monitoring and evaluating a new reading program in their early elementary school.

Davies finally asked, what purposes does citizen participation serve in the schools? Davies suggests that if people are involved in building and maintaining a program it becomes to some extent theirs—they own it. Hence, citizen involvement can mean mobilization of support for schools. Citizens are also resources or help for schools in a number of ways. They can not only influence decision making but legitimate it as well. Finally, citizen participation benefits the participants themselves, giving them a sense of purpose with regard to the program as well as a sense of efficacy and status.

Davies was addressing the above points to an audience of professional educators, to enlighten them as to the advantages of citizen participation. I would sum up these concepts under the interlinked ideas that citizens gain a sense of control over their lives as they participate and learn how change can occur; and they represent an essential resource in educating children that cannot be duplicated in school.

Not all citizens want to participate at a maximum level, say, to sit on a school council that governs the personnel, budget, and curriculum matters of the school. Davies lists multiple ways that citizens might participate, some of which have been mentioned (1981, pp. 83–119). The matter for have-nots is urgent, however; they must do what is necessary to improve their schools for their children. Control and power, enough to bring about change, are their objectives. They cannot afford time for bake sales and PTA meetings. I should allow, however, that the other five functions—authorizing, enabling, service-giving, planning, and evaluating—may have to be means that citizens use to gain access to and information about the school. There will nonetheless be a hierarchy in the functions of citizen participation in education, with priority going to governing as an ultimate function.

With rare exceptions, community members, parents especially, do not want to run the schools; they wish ultimately to rest in the belief that the schools are under control. Normally, most parents have enough to do without seeking to make policy for an enterprise about whose operation they know relatively little. Over time, parents have become accustomed to leaving the control of the school to those paid to operate it. As noted earlier, many have come to see the school as a delivery system and themselves as passive consumers. Governing surfaces as a top priority only in those cases where it is painfully obvious to parents, children, and other citizens that the school is not being operated to the advantage of its students.

This discussion of the meanings of citizen participation in education would not be complete without reference to studies of the effects of the involvement of low-income and minority parents in their schools. Weinberg (1983, pp. 246–56) summarized several studies in the following conclusions:

1. School efforts to educate parents to teach their children may be based on too simple a model; the entire ecology of the child—including the school—must be considered.
2. Neither the residential mobility of low-income families nor the absence of the father is related to, and therefore an explanation of, low achievement by poor children.
3. In black neighborhoods, the more the schools tried to involve parents and other community members in decision making, the better the achievement in a sample of sixth graders in twenty Los Angeles elementary schools.
4. The relation between the educational level of parents and their support for their children's achievement in school is very weak.
5. In black schools, parent involvement in the classroom, not just in the school, is significantly related to gains in student achievement scores.
6. Parent involvement in both Head Start and Follow Through is positively correlated with student achievement gains.

These conclusions suggest that appropriate parent involvement can have beneficial effects on their children's school learning outcomes. But what are appropriate vehicles or forms of such collective involvement? We turn now to a systematic analysis of linkage forms between schools and their neighborhoods.

THEORETICAL FORMS OF SCHOOL-COMMUNITY LINKAGE

Litwak and Meyer (1974) systematically categorized ways that schools could create links with their communities. This analysis included the fact that in many neighborhoods there are preexisting organizations interested in the school, both single-issue groups (education) and multi-issue groups. Their presentation consisted of a theoretical overview of local school-community relations, administrative styles, primary groups, and linking mechanisms, and an analysis of the pros and cons of each of these linking mechanisms.

Their entire work rested on what they termed a "balance theory" of school-community relations, which represented a compromise between closed- and open-door approaches (pp. 5–6). A school with a closed-door approach to the community maintains a large social distance from parents and allows them, at best, the spectator role, as mentioned earlier. The open-door position assumes that students learn a great deal beyond school doors in their families, peer groups, and neighborhoods. It is connected with a "student-centered" philosophy of education and encourages parent involvement in all phases of the school process.

The balance theory, in turn, rests on a distinction the authors make between expert and nonexpert tasks required in education. The myriad forms of nurturance of children in families are said to be nonexpert tasks; contrariwise, the teaching of reading and mathematics, for example, is an expert task. Under the balance approach, parents stick to providing the nonexpert tasks; the staff, the expert. The authors were aware of the pitfalls of making a dichotomy between the two, since teachers must perform nonexpert tasks, especially in the affective areas of motivation and discipline, and parents may tutor their children in homework. Nonetheless, successful linkage, they assert, is grounded in recognition of the differentiation of these roles.

Another distinction they make acknowledges the difference between the school as a bureaucratic form, in which social relationships are impersonal, instrumental, specialized, and oriented toward the production of uniform outcomes, and the family as a primary group, in which social relations are personal, more generalized, and oriented toward an idiosyncratic or nonuniform outcome (that is, the rearing of this particular child). This distinction between uniform and nonuniform is not evaluative of either but recognizes that such differences pose dangers in communication. Therefore, any school-community linkage mechanism must contribute to a balance between the two sides that respects the contribution of the other to the whole child.

Ways the School Can Link with the Community

Since Litwak and Meyer's intended audience was school personnel interested in creating viable links with the neighborhood, their discussion is skewed toward initiatives by the school. The linking mechanisms they describe are: detached worker, opinion leader, auxiliary volunteer association, settlement house, common messengers, mass media, formal authority, and delegated function.

The detached worker is a professional person with autonomy from the school who is "in" the community to establish trusting relations with parents, children, and other community members with a view toward enhancing the school in their eyes. Sara Lightfoot (1983) described the experiences of three such workers, ministerial interns, who lived in the Carver High School attendance district of Atlanta. The opinion leader is an established neighborhood leader utilized by the school to influence residents. The most typical case is the use of such persons in mounting millage campaigns.

The auxiliary voluntary association is a group that draws its membership from both school and neighborhood. Typical examples are parent-teacher associations and homeroom mothers' clubs. The settlement house is a community center that incorporates educational and therapeutic programs. Some early community school programs embodied this concept, which sought more influence on the young, through afternoon and evening programming, than school provided. Common messengers are persons who have membership in both areas; they function as messengers between home and school. Children are most commonly thought of this way, but the concept can include indigenous workers, regular parent volunteers, or even members of local boards of education.

Using the mass media, the school organization informs the community through newspapers, TV, radio, leaflets, or newsletters. The formal authority is a person with some position of formal power who influences (coerces?) community members with regard to school requirements. An example might be an attendance officer or a principal who suspends a student. Finally, the delegated function is not a direct linkage mechanism as were the seven previous types. Rather, the school delegates a function to another agency that is linked to the community. For example, the school may refer a student to a medical agency. Harry L. Summerfield (1971) described a merger between a public elementary school and a social service agency (a neighborhood house) in a low-income neighborhood. Each institution cooperated with the other in serving the same clientele.

Litwak and Meyer evaluate these linking mechanisms using four criteria:

1. The degree of organizational initiative required
2. The degree of intensity required in the communication process

3. The amount of focused expertise necessary
4. The scope of the mechanism to reach the maximum number of people.

For example, the detached worker mechanism requires great school initiative. The school must fund the position and then find and send forth an acceptable candidate. It also allows intense relationships between the worker and the community, within which he focuses his expertise, for example, on correcting misperceptions residents may have of the school. The mechanism has only limited scope, though, since the worker can deal with only a few people at a time. On the other hand, the mass media have great scope as a linking mechanism, and can reach a great number of people, but little initiative or intensity is required on the school's part and little focused expertise is provided. The mechanism of the child as a common messenger scores moderately well on initiative, intensity, and scope, but again it provides little focused expertise.

The authors then examine how these mechanisms might be employed in sequences and combinations, depending on whether the schools operated on the closed-door, open-door, or balance theories; but here we are concerned with inner-city schools, where there is likely to be a large social distance between home and school. In this case, the authors suggest, the best mechanisms—should school officials wish to close that distance (a highly speculative hypothesis)—would be the detached worker and the settlement house. Use of the opinion leader, the voluntary auxiliary association, and the common messenger can at most achieve moderate closure of the gap. Heavy reliance on the mass media and formal authority guarantees maintenance or even further widening of the social gap.

Ways the Community Can Link with the School

Litwak and Meyer are not unaware of the problem of inner-city schools:

> The civil rights movement and national concern for education of the "underprivileged" have dramatized the racial, ethnic, and social biases of many schools. School systems and individual schools become rigid and unapproachable in some instances, and a few may even be corrupt in the sense of deliberately blocking the public purposes for which they were established. (p. 33)

Given that the school may not be interested in establishing two-way communication between itself and the neighborhood, the authors turn to consideration of how the community might employ linking mechanisms, described below: advocate bureaucracy, strategic influences, voluntary association, mass media, ad hoc demonstrations, sustained collective action, common messenger, and individual ad hoc contact.

The advocate bureaucracy, though similar to the school's mechanism of "delegated function," or use of a second agency, takes on a different meaning when the community employs it to intervene in its behalf. Examples given are the NAACP or the ACLU. This advocate agency could be an established group such as a labor union, an ethnic association, or a political organization that serves the community interest on an ongoing basis, or it could be a group that serves temporarily and for a limited purpose, such as a law firm. It may simply provide information to its clients, participate with residents in advocacy actions, or act on its clients' behalf. Clearly, though the authors do not mention them, neighborhood organizations are, or can be, examples of this mechanism.

Strategic influences are the third parties who can influence the school. They may be insiders in the school bureaucracy or powerful persons outside it. They are the analogue to the opinion leaders that the school might employ as linkage mechanisms. Saul Alinsky provided an example of how to use a strategic influencer when he acknowledged in a 1972 *Playboy* interview (1972a, p. 74) that he had secretly enlisted Mayor Edward Kelly's help in winning a contract with Chicago's meat packers for the union that was part of his Back of the Yards Council during the late 1930s and the early 1940s.

The voluntary association may be PTAs, continuing or ad hoc parents' education groups, or multipurpose neighborhood associations (the authors do not use this last phrase). The community has little control of the mass media, but through their associations they may exert some influence. Advocate bureaucracies or voluntary associations occasionally employ the media or create newsworthy events, such as are exemplified in the next two mechanisms. Ad hoc demonstrations are publicized marches, outdoor mass meetings, sit-ins, disruptions of meetings, sporadic violent or destructive acts, which all involve attempts to direct collective behavior. Sustained collective action would be strikes, boycotts, and other forms of harrassment that may attract public attention to the group's cause and interfere with the target organization's functioning. This type of action assumes a broad-based, cohesive community organization.

The common messenger is a category that includes indigenous employees, volunteers, both expert (such as teachers) and nonexpert (street-crossing guards, for example), or other volunteers among parents and other residents. They may be low-powered, as are children, or high-powered, as in the case of indigenous members of the school board. Finally, there is the individual ad hoc contact. The classic example here is the parent who contacts the teacher to complain or to get information. Its effectiveness is determined by the purpose of the contact (whether on behalf of a specific child or the student body in general), its timing (crisis situation or not), its frequency, its form (in person, in writing, or by telephone), and the formal position in the school hierarchy of the person contacted.

Litwak and Meyer again utilize the four criteria by which they judged school attempts at linking with the community. The first is the degree of initiative required. To confront the ability of the bureaucracy to listen selectively or to "tune out" altogether, the community must draw together the resources of a counter- (or advocate) bureaucracy, an effort demanding much greater initiative than comparable high-initiative actions by the schools.

The second criterion was primary group intensity, the counterpart of initiative. In other words, how intensely should the mechanism be applied in order to convey the message successfully? Where social distance is great, as it almost always is in the schools we are considering, great intensity will be required.

The third criterion was focused expertise. It has also been noted that schools engage in both expert and nonexpert services for children. Parents, viewed as nonexperts, may be able to confront directly school personnel over nonexpert issues, such as discipline of children, but they may need the aid of experts or even the support of an expert advocacy agency to confront the school on expert issues. Often the issue involves both expert and nonexpert aspects. Hiring a competent teacher (expert) who shares community values (nonexpert) has been a common example.

The fourth criterion was scope. Initially, parents might think in terms of the broadest possible publication of their cause, but the issue may be such that other parents or community groups may object to and oppose the initiative. The mechanism to be employed must be considered in the light of the context.

Other Variables in the School-Community Linkage

Litwak and Meyer combine three intervening variables in the analysis. The first considers whether the school bureaucracy is friendly or hostile; the second, whether the majority of the neighborhood residents supports the local community group or not; the third, which administrative style is operative in the school.

The school may be overtly hostile to the community or indifferent, which is a form of hostility betokened by insensitivity. Under these conditions, even if most neighborhood residents support the community group's organizing, it will require high initiative, intensity, and wide scope. The issue determines the need for focused expertise in the group's tactics. Litwak and Meyer assert that if it is of an expert nature (expert at developing content for a black studies course, for example), the group may require the assistance of an advocate bureaucracy. If it is low in expertise requirements (such as demanding inclusion of a prepackaged sex education course in the curriculum), the group itself can confront the school directly. When the expert and nonexpert aspects of the proposal are equally important, as in the demand for hiring competent teachers who share the community's values, a mixture of strategies together with appeals to influencers (influential third parties) is the best approach.

The administrative style of a school can be a determinant of the community's tactics. Litwak and Meyer list several types of such styles, ranging along a continuum. On the one end is the rationalistic style, which advocates hierarchy of authority, specialization of function, impersonal relations, and assignment of personnel by merit. This style, according to the authors, is best addressed by an expert advocacy bureaucracy. At the other end is the human relations style, characterized by child-centeredness, a generalized curriculum, personal interactions, and also assignment by merit. This style is said to be most vulnerable to a tactic of direct approach to individual teachers or a group of them. Expert knowledge is much less essential in the community group, say Litwak and Meyer, when the human relations style is prevalent. Probably such human relations schools are even rarer in inner-city neighborhoods than are the rationalistic, but both are found in well-run schools that are amenable to change, even though they are polar opposites.

The remaining five styles represent corruptions of the first two in some fashion. The compartmentalized style, for example, combines elements of the first two, that is, the school's organization and scheduling appears rationalistic, but individual classrooms are characterized by the human relations style. The laissez-faire style determines goals and objectives not according to a priori rules but in an ad hoc fashion.[1] A nepotistic style is characterized by a "pervasive infusion of nonmerit criteria" in assignment of personnel (Litwak & Meyer, 1974, p. 63).

Since organizational objectives do not govern staff under these conditions, they may be oriented toward their personal self-interest (working conditions, salary, benefits) rather than toward educational goals. When this mode predominates, decisions and task performance are likely to reflect personal convenience at the expense of effective education. Under the autocratic and paternalistic styles, the principal is the "captain of the ship." The autocrat is less restrained by rules and is likely to assign personnel using nonmerit considerations. The paternalistic principal emphasizes personal relations among staff. Where the principal is a strong central figure, change tactics should probably be directed at him or her; where forms of the human relations style are apparent, staff members could probably be confronted directly with success.

The authors admit the probability of combinations of style. Nonetheless, these "ideal" types add considerably to Summerfield's (1971, p. 93) generic contention that the principal's style will tend to fit the school-community context. Summerfield's study will be discussed in Chapter 9.

Evaluating the Community's Use of School-Initiated Linking Mechanisms

Litwak and Meyer delineated the advantages and disadvantages of each mechanism the community could use to link with the school. The detached worker, employed by the neighborhood organization, could represent the neighborhood's interests to the school and would work mostly among neighborhood residents on whatever school-related problems arose. This worker, knowledgeable about the system— such as a former teacher—could function sometimes as an ombudsman and at other times as an organizer to generate collective action. Although the authors see the detached worker as an advocate representing the community's educational interests, the worker will be far more effective organizing people to assert themselves rather than speaking for them.

The authors' discussion of opinion leaders does not distinguish types of leaders in low-income neighborhoods.[2] Yet their discussion of community use of its own opinion leaders to promote school change raises a couple of interesting questions. First, does the leader have effective backing?[3] In a cohesive representative neighborhood organization, the answer would be yes. But second and more fundamentally, how would a neighborhood organization opinion leader influence a bureaucracy? Although this person might not be technically trained, he or she could mobilize the community for protest and pressure to accept independent expert advocates. The opinion leader might also be able to contact and influence opinion leaders within the bureaucracy. Although Litwak and Meyer suggest that the opinion leader mechanism is of limited usefulness to the community because of a lack of technical knowledge, they seriously understate the importance of such leaders in mobilizing the community for school change. These people are the heart of a successful neighborhood organization.

The settlement house concept sees the school as a center for adult activity, as well as that of children, supervised by experts for the benefit of the children's education. In a utopian scenario, the school is the site of regular meetings in which parents' study groups meet with professional educators to "develop ways of motivating and helping their children academically" (p. 206). The authors admit this mechanism is the most difficult of all for the community to initiate on its own; but if the neighborhood organization were sufficiently developed— with its own meeting facility and staff—it could invite professionals to engage in this activity on its own turf, or it could pressure for such meetings at the school.

The voluntary association appears as the best vehicle for the community to employ as an agent of change with regard to schools.

> Almost at once after formation, the voluntary association can become a base for political pressure and the development of economic resources. Persistence, growth, and considerably increased resources, together with organizational capacity to employ personnel, allow the voluntary association to move toward becoming an organization capable of using experts as the community's own advocate bureaucracy. (p. 234)

Despite this hopeful statement, Litwak and Meyer devote the rest of their discussion to why such organizations in poor neighborhoods are unlikely to come into existence and to endure. Yet they state that their own studies of family structures in the poorest neighborhoods revealed a wide diversity: "homogeneity of social pathology in low income urban neighborhoods—broken families, many children, unemployment, and the like—just did not appear" (p. 236). Where such diversity exists, potential leaders and members of a multipurpose neighborhood organization also exist.

The mass media can be used by the community very effectively to influence the school. They are only a handmaiden to the neighborhood organization, however, and their use is always dictated by the context. It is often difficult if not impossible to control the outcome of such use, and control depends to a large extent upon the capacity, that is, the power, of the organization.

The common messenger approach when used by the community has often taken the form of employment of indigenous persons by the school, filling of positions on school boards by neighborhood residents, or monitoring school performance by neighborhood watchdog committees. If taken to one extreme, this approach could deny the necessity for expertise in the educational enterprise, state Litwak and Meyer, in remaining consistent with their balance theory. The common messenger, they hold, will be most fruitful in the nonexpert areas, though these could include input on personnel, curriculum, and budgeting decisions. In general, this mechanism will work best when it facilitates two-way communication and when agreement and mutual trust are sufficient to keep stress low. If the common messenger has expert knowledge in education, all other things being equal, so much the better.

The delegated function mechanism could be very useful to the neighborhood organization, especially when it must deal with the bureaucracy on technical matters. Either the community can borrow a bureaucracy to influence the school, say, a law firm or the NAACP, to deal with districting policy, or it could develop its own bureaucracy. The first case requires that the interests of community and outside bureaucracy coincide if the coalition is to succeed. The second encounters the problems of organization building in a low-income neighborhood, not the least of which is a long time-line.

SOME PROBLEMS WITH THE THEORY OF LINKING MECHANISMS

There are shortcomings in this elaborate theoretical work of Litwak and Meyer on school-community relations. One, for example, is the real difficulty community groups experience in assessing what is wrong and what to do about it. The last chapter of this book expands on the matter of problem assessment. Furthermore, strategies (unfortunately labeled linking mechanisms) are not recipes to be slavishly or simplistically followed. They are not simply blocks to be stacked up until their weight breaks the resistance of the opposition. Experienced organizers know better:

> They have a far more complicated effect. They can change the ways in which our members see themselves and the ways in which they are willing to participate in the organization. They affect how our opposition

sees us . . . They also influence public opinion, which in turn helps determine what coalitions and alliances we are able to build. (Kahn, 1982, p. 188)

Another criticism has to do with terminology. Litwak and Meyer provide few examples in their analysis, which leaves the meanings of some terms open to interpretation. This problem becomes particularly acute in delineating the differences between expert and nonexpert, technical and nontechnical, uniform and nonuniform. It will be dealt with below in a separate subsection.

A related difficulty lies in the authors' conception of balance theory. It may be interpreted as tantamount to "leaving the education to the educators and the parenting to the parents." Litwak and Meyer acknowledge that there is no real dichotomy, but they do not emphasize enough the tendency of educators to take this position. The psychological acceptance of this balance is at best an end state, not a condition to be assumed at the beginning of the school-community relationship.

Another shortcoming lies in not pursuing the implications of a basic insight far enough. The authors caution that not only is there a lack of sufficient advocate bureaucracies in our society upon which citizens may call for help, but in addition, "programs initiated from the community in our society are especially likely to generate conflict" (p. 52). Yet they discuss this profound insight no further. Urban school officials, of course, are aware of this probability and initiate enough activity to bank community fires and prevent them from raging out of control. Summerfield, in fact, states that this is the principal's main political role (1971, p. 93).

The authors also assume that a neighborhood organization's capacity to promote school change is correlated with the type of neighborhood it is in. Middle-class neighborhoods, they think, have the greatest potential to organize for change in schools; traditional (ethnic) neighborhoods will only organize to oppose change; volatile neighborhoods, wherein neighborhood groups oppose one another, will have little capacity; and mass neighborhoods, characterized by no internal networks (a fictitious ideal type), will have no capacity. While low-income neighborhoods do have greater obstacles to overcome, they have demonstrated organizational capacity. To the authors' credit, they acknowledge that if a school wishes to develop linkages with its low-income neighborhood, it should support those mechanisms that raise neighborhood resource levels, such as multipurpose neighborhood organizations (p. 147).

The Problem of Technical Knowledge

A great deal of the social distance between the educator and the low-income neighborhood resident, especially minority parents, is due not to the educator's arcane knowledge of the teaching/learning process or of subject matter but to social class differences, particularly status. What the neighborhood people must come to realize is that the educators' claim to professional status is rooted not in subject matter, since they are simply not experts there. Rather their claim to professionalism is based on their presumed special understanding of how to teach youngsters in groups. As most educational psychologists understand, however, teaching is art as well as science. The point to be taken is that, to the extent that teaching is an art, it forever eludes being the preserve of special technique alone. Where one teacher is better than another is usually in this intangible, subjective, but important realm of the artistic. This area refers not so much to ability to perform as to ability to understand and construct complex human relationships. This creative process requires observational skill, insight, patience, and flexibility, in addition to intelligence, self-awareness, and self-confidence. Hence, neat distinctions between expert and nonexpert are impossible to draw.

Nevertheless, school staff can heighten the social distance between themselves and working-class parents by emphasizing that what they teach and how they teach it is beyond the understanding of parents; therefore, parents should stay out of the whole process. The recurring suggestion by Litwak and Meyer that on expert matters the parents need an expert advocate should draw attention to the fact that it is the school staff who define what is an expert or technical area and what is not. When the parents and their neighborhood organization confront the school, they must design approaches that take this high ground away from the school where possible. They must redefine the issue in effect so that they can be seen as competent to engage the school in constructive dialogue.

Ron Edmonds (1983), a major contemporary advocate for the creation of effective inner-city schools, gave an example of how parents wishing to improve their school might take away the technical high ground from the school: A group concerned about the disproportionate number of suspensions of black male children should develop a baseline of data from several schools. Since the suspension rate will vary dramatically from school to school, the group can approach school officials with a specific question:

What is there about you and your colleagues that prevents you from doing just as well as those people over there who also work in the public schools? They work under analogous conditions and yet they've been able to make a difference. I want you to explain to me why you can't duplicate their results. (p. 24)

In this case, redefining the issue means placing the technical burden on the school experts. The organization, using the schools' own data, can pressure them to live by their own rules.

In discussing theoretical forms of citizen participation and collective school-community linkage, this chapter has sought to underscore the potential effectiveness of the neighborhood organization to promote urban school change. The next chapter examines studies of such interaction.

9

Lessons from Case Studies
of Organizing

*Time, and our children, are on our side. If we are willing to
choke back our fears, we may find a way to fight the system.
And as our children watch us fight for them, we may learn
that we have educated our kids and beaten the system—
despite the odds. (Lurie, 1970, p. 267)*

Study of failure as well as of success can be instructive. This
chapter draws together a number of case studies of organizing for
urban school reform, in order to develop the guidelines or principles
an organization seeking such reform must keep in mind. Two contrasting cases of parents acting collectively out of anger against their
elementary school reveal that the emotions parents feel that stem from
their children's schooling experience are a necessary but not sufficient
ingredient in organizing. A major study (Gittell, 1980) of the limits of
community organizations in confronting big city school systems draws
criticism for its inadequacies. A brief examination of two other studies
demonstrates the problems that follow from not achieving a consensus
on goals among parents and other residents. The chapter then reviews
an extensive study of factors in contrasting neighborhood political
styles vis-à-vis public schools. Finally, the conclusions (lessons) are
listed.

ORGANIZING PARENTAL ANGER

Anger is essential. Without such passion, under control, organizing
will lack its driving energy; but anger alone is not enough. The two
examples of collective outbursts of parental anger toward the system
that follow instruct us that reflection and feedback of patient, long-
term organizing efforts are essential if the parents' efforts are not to
lead to failure.

The first case occurred during the spring of 1965 at the Christopher Gibson School in the black North Dorchester section of Boston (Lukas, 1985). The former Rhodes scholar, Jonathan Kozol, had just been fired in his first year of teaching fourth grade. He had been having the children study the poetry of Langston Hughes instead of the system-prescribed stories about Miss Molly, Fluffy Tail, and Miss Valentine. Some of the parents of children in this school had met to discuss the awful conditions chronicled later by Kozol himself in his best-selling exposé, *Death at an Early Age* (1967), but they had taken no action. When word of Kozol's firing reached them, however, their anger boiled over. Workers from the Congress of Racial Equality (CORE), a national black civil rights organization with a local in Boston, had knocked on parents' doors to inform them of the bad news and to urge them to attend a rally at a local church. Two hundred showed up.

The following Monday, sit-ins and pickets began at Gibson to protest Kozol's firing and the conditions in the building. Many parents also kept their children at home during this time, one of many school boycott tactics used during this era. Their demands included his reinstatement, elimination of the rattan (a whip for disciplining children), up-to-date integrated textbooks, elimination of basement and auditorium classrooms, and more respectful treatment of parents and children by staff. Tension escalated after a meeting two days later between Deputy Superintendent Marguerite Sullivan and fifteen mothers, who refused to leave the building. Boston's School Committee, which was dominated by Irish working-class interests, interceded in the person of Thomas Eisenstadt, who promised to conduct a full investigation of the Kozol affair if the sit-in would end. It did. The promised report came several weeks later, exonerating the school of any blame, to no one's surprise. But by then summer had arrived, school was out, and the parents had other things to worry about.

The second case occurred in 1979 in the rural town of Memphis, Michigan (Tofani, 1985). It was rumored among the parents of children in his seventh-grade class that Edward Stachura was teaching deviant sexual values. Some said he showed drawings of sexual organs and pictures of his wife having a baby. He advocated abortion if one's baby were deformed, they claimed. He talked about nudity in his family, they had heard. Thirty outraged parents showed up at a school-board meeting shortly after these rumors began, demanding that he be fired. Astonished and unprepared for the fury of these parents, the board suspended him with pay.

Stachura, in turn, brought suit in federal district court. He argued that he had been denied due process and his constitutional rights. The pictures of his wife, his new baby, and himself were not sexually explicit, only shots of heads and shoulders to demonstrate to male students that there were alternatives to going out and getting drunk when their (future) wives were giving birth. He had said only that abortion was an alternative if the fetus was discovered malformed; many such fetuses are spontaneously aborted. Discussion of nudity in his family arose when one of his students anonymously placed in the question box he provided for student questions a picture from a *National Geographic* showing a woman wearing only a grass skirt. He had pointed out that the definition of nudity was culturally determined, that his own children had run around the house naked until they grew older and learned that our society does not accept such behavior.

A jury not only reinstated Stachura but also ordered the school district to pay $321,000 in damages, $31,000 of which was to come from the pockets of the school-board members and the superintendent themselves. Although the award is still under appeal, Stachura has become a withdrawn, timid teacher, fearful of any creative or innovative encounters with his students. He has been ruined as an effective teacher in that district.

These two cases point out several hazards in simply venting blasts of parental anger at schools. In the first, parents were justified in their anger. They had done their homework in investigating conditions in their children's school. The precipitating incident of Kozol's firing led to their taking direct action. However, once they had taken their best shot, which appeared easily absorbed by the racist school system, they had no longer-term strategy to fall back on, no organizational base to keep issues alive. It had taken years of neglect to achieve the chaos that was the Christopher Gibson School; it would not be rectified in a few days. Because their demands were clear, tangible, and reasonable, they assumed that underlying school structures and values would support their acceptance. This was their error. School personnel denied that their charges had any validity, because these people were enmeshed in the patronage system. That is, most of the principals, teachers, custodians, and other workers in the system retained their jobs by making regular large ($250–$500) contributions to school committee members' campaigns. Not to make such contributions was to risk being demoted or losing one's job.

This patronage system in Boston rendered it even less amenable to change than civil service reformed systems of other cities. Even slight inroads by minorities or non-Irish white groups represented major threats to the existence of patronage. An established community organization would have understood that redress would only be successful if it included the long-range assistance of powerful third parties, especially the federal courts, to topple the patronage system. Although patronage was a complicating factor in the Boston case, urban systems are not very malleable. In fact, Milwaukee's system was relatively unscathed a few years later by widespread boycotts of public schools by blacks seeking an end to de facto segregation and its attendant evils of inferior school buildings, programs, and instruction.

In the second case, the parents had not investigated the actual conditions of the classroom but had relied solely on rumor and innuendo. In addition, they confronted a small-town system that was eminently movable. The board was a pushover because its members were neighbors who wanted to do what their friends thought right. Ironically, the teacher in this case was probably an asset to the school, though it is not clear whether in frank discussion with the parents, he and they would have ultimately agreed on the proper approach to sex education. The parents in this situation were ill informed and "won" their victory, which led to an outcome arguably as bad for their children as the case of the Boston parents who were well informed but lost their battle. This incident, critics might say, is one in which regular communication between parents and teachers might have been sufficient. But in cities regular open communication is not achieved by merely going to the school for a chat, as might be the case in a small town. It is the outcome of extensive organizing. In the Memphis case, the value to the parents of a neighborhood organization would not be to enable them to battle their way to victory but to help them research their perceived problem and reflect on it before acting precipitously. In the Boston case, the organization would be the institutional advocate of the parents and children; in the Memphis case, it would act as an educator itself, an instructor of its own members. These are the two functions of the neighborhood organization as mediating institution: external advocate and internal educator.

In summary, the Boston and Memphis parent confrontations teach that parental anger, even though organized and fierce, is not sufficient as a force for school improvement. Parents need a long-term, neighborhood-oriented organizational base that will not only help them advocate their cause over several years, if need be, but will also bring them to consensus about the meaning of school improvement. This latter function implies parent education.

AVOIDING DESPAIR: A CRITIQUE OF A MAJOR STUDY

Perhaps the best-known study of the effects of community organizations on big city public schools was conducted under the leadership of Marilyn Gittell (1980) during the late 1970s. Entitled *Limits of Citizen Participation: The Decline of Community Organizations*, it concluded gloomily that these organizations had not been able to bring about structural change in their school systems. Yet the study contains several shortcomings.

The study chose three large cities, Boston, Atlanta, and Los Angeles, as sites for the operation of sixteen citizen organizations. Four of these organizations were not low-income. Seven others, although low-income, were mandated into existence by government fiat, though one in Los Angeles, fictitiously named Margaritas, was mandated after Chicano students boycotted three high schools, demanding changes. The remaining five, discussed below as most closely approximating the type of organization emphasized in this book, included three in Atlanta (the Braves, Grits, and Magnolias), one in Boston (the Celtics), and a fifth in Los Angeles (the Sunsets). Yet none of them organized effectively to reform their public schools.

By the criteria developed earlier in describing self-initiated multipurpose neighborhood organizations in low-income areas, only one of the sixteen appears to be of this nature. The Braves of Atlanta was at first (1967) a settlement house funded by the Episcopal Church. It ran programs dealing with welfare rights, tenants' rights, health issues, prison reform, and political activism. Although its leader was well known, the organization was seen as disruptive in its tactics. The residents, low-income blacks, viewed the organization as one of the few groups that represented their interests. The Braves had participated in the development stage of the 1973 compromise on desegregation in Atlanta, but its membership was listed as citywide rather than from a particular neighborhood.

The Grits' principal involvement with the schools was through the provision of alternative education services for dropouts and potential dropouts. Again, although it is located in a tightly knit poor white nieghborhood just outside Atlanta's downtown and is primarily oriented toward local economic development activities, such as cottage industries and planning input to City Hall, the study lists its membership also as citywide. The Magnolias did not appear involved in any way with school issues except through individuals seeking positions of leadership in the system.

None of these three were listed as spending any time on school system issues and minimal time (0–10 percent) on alternative education issues. These percentages were based on site researchers' notes taken at organization meetings. The vast majority of time at these meetings was taken up with organization maintenance, especially in the provision of social services. The Celtics of Boston appear to be a community development corporation, not a neighborhood organization in the sense used in this book. The Sunsets of Los Angeles was primarily an information center for Chicano parents; its function was service, not advocacy.

Two flaws are thus apparent in the study. First, it is not clear in what way, if any, these sixteen organizations are representative of the population of community organizations. One could get the impression that there are few if any neighborhood organizations of the type described in Chapter 7 in these cities. Yet there is at least one powerful Alinsky organization in Los Angeles that was not mentioned. Second, it appears as though the self-initiated low-income organizations in effect never dealt with the school system or only did so marginally. Lack of activity does not warrant the conclusion that such groups are not capable of influencing system policy; this point needs further discussion.

Implicit in the study is the assumption that organizational form and function are class-based. Low-income advocacy organizations, the study claimed, "have abandoned their advocate roles and have become part of the system or have accepted funding which has increased their dependence on external sources" (p. 66). Again, the study asserts that "in lower income communities there is a lack of political-action-directed organizations, coupled with frustration over or disinterest in school issues" (p. 241). This denial of the efficacy of such organizations is not only an assumption, but is strangely dissonant with the obvious concern by the research staff for increasing opportunities for low-income citizens, especially for participation in school policymaking. While there is pressure on any low-income neighborhood organization to provide services instead of to advocate on behalf of the residents, numerous cases cited throughout this book document the retention of militancy despite pressures for services.[1]

This tendency in the research design to dichotomize organizational features is a third flaw. Community organizations were characterized by economic dimension (low income versus middle to upper income); by racial/ethnic criteria (black, Hispanic, other); by leadership type (rotating; mandated, that is, externally imposed by an institution such as a court, school district, or federal grantor; constant, which implies virtually nonexistent membership; and staff leadership); by strategies employed (service, advocacy, or advisory); by geographic focus (citywide or neighborhood); and by whether the group itself was mandated into existence or was self-initiated. One could be led erroneously into thinking that the only organizations that exist in low-to-moderate-income neighborhoods were those that were of the settlement house or community development corporation variety. The study's approach to analysis not only created oversimplified categories but also ignored the idiosyncratic events and personalities that experienced activists might learn from.

Principal among the conclusions reached by Gittell and her associates was that community organizations among the affluent are freer to play advocacy roles with respect to the public school system because their leadership is not constrained by demands from constituents for social services and by economic hardships. In general, the affluent groups were deemed more influential than the low-income groups by a poll of neighborhood and citywide leaders, because they could retain a militant stance and their leadership rotated or changed, allowing for greater investment by more citizens in the process of change. Mandated groups were less influential than self-initiated ones. But none of these groups was seen as able to bring about structural change in the school systems. All citizen input in the three cities was at the discretion of the local administrators. Although forms of administrative decentralization existed in all three cities, local administrators had no independent decision-making powers. Citizens in these regions had even less power to influence decisions affecting their neighborhoods.

No explanation was given in the study as to why the multi-issue low-income groups paid little attention to educational issues, except that they were fully occupied with housing and economic development issues. Another possible reason, not mentioned, is that such hard-pressed organizations have not known how to institutionalize themselves into the policymaking process, short of demanding it. Some, however, BUILD in Buffalo, for example, have demonstrated exquisite political sophistication.

The Gittell study, on the face of it, is both unsettling and unsatisfying. Although the conclusions ring true—especially that there are serious limitations on low-income neighborhood organizations, and citizen participation more generally—the study's pessimism is too complete. It does reveal trends that pose obstacles to an organization's success. Internally they include

1. The tendency to move toward service and away from advocacy under pressure from external funding sources and internal member needs
2. The tendency of some leaders to try to use funds for their personal use, from landing jobs to covert theft

Externally, these obstacles include the tendency of school systems to avoid cooperation and the problem of goal displacement (which is explored in the next chapter) as organizations seek to exert control rather than promote program quality.

Yet the study ignores the success of these groups, as well as of numerous other groups, in other directions, such as housing and public infrastructure improvement, economic redevelopment, recreation program additions, and crime prevention. Other studies indicate that success with schools involves a number of factors, chief of which is setting reasonable goals.

SETTING GOALS FOR ORGANIZING

How do the neighborhood organization and the parent body define influence as a goal? The following case illustrates how a campaign for control of a neighborhood's public schools fell short. The Woodlawn Organization (TWO), a prototypical Alinsky organization in Chicago's southside Woodlawn community, a low-income black neighborhood, attempted in the mid-1960s to assert control over two local elementary public schools (Fish, 1973).

TWO had no leverage with the school board until the University of Chicago, TWO's neighbor to the north, sought a ten million dollar grant to create a research center involving the two schools. TWO sought and achieved creation of a 21-member board that would oversee the project. The school board, the university, and TWO each placed seven members on it. Thus constituted, the Woodlawn Experimental Schools Project (WESP) applied for and received a $1.35 million federal grant to upgrade the two schools and initiate a community planning process. Even though TWO was not interested in innovation so much as in control of the project, it never gained authority over the school staff, who dragged their feet and obstructed the project whenever they could. The governing partnership that had started out began to crumble.

Without the authority to initiate change and restructure relationships within the school system, WESP became more like a community organization and less like a city agency, more the educational division of TWO and less the Board of Education's demonstration project. (Fish, 1973, p. 230)

The governing partnership, in other words, had never been achieved, and given the drive for control by TWO and the recalcitrance of the powerful system to admit TWO's influence, each side reverted to form. "The intent to demonstrate possibilities of community control was subverted," wrote Fish (p. 230), because no public system is going to abdicate its control to a community group, no matter how representative. What the neighborhood group should seek is shared power, institutionalization into policymaking processes. The search for community control is goal displacement from the more realistic goal of sharing control.

This case also introduces the notion of "political slack," which is related to setting reasonable goals. Robert Dahl (1960) coined this term with reference to the flexibility of a given urban system to absorb change without losing its control. Some urban school systems may be so rigid, defensive, and inaccessible that they give little or no heed to citizen demands for input. Boston and Atlanta in the Gittell study might fit this extreme. Los Angeles, however, through its emphasis on school advisory councils, appeared to give more credence to the citizens' voice. All three remained structurally unchanged, nonetheless, in the face of citizen demands. In the Chicago case, the system did allow a strong community organization leeway to create programs that led to boosts in student achievement scores and parent participation, because—at least initially—this effort did not appear to threaten the school board's ultimate control. But TWO's demands for the transfer of recalcitrant teachers and principals was a threat to the professional establishment. At this point the doors of access slammed shut. Thus, the threat that the community organization appears to pose to control by the system seems in inverse proportion to the success the organization can have in school program revitalization. There is probably some point of balance, then, between threat and efficacy.

Another case related to goal confusion occurred in the Eastown area of Grand Rapids, Michigan (Williams, 1980). The Sigsbee Park (public) Elementary School, which enrolled 360 children, was a stereotypical inner-city school. Its parents were predominantly low to moderate in income, its student population was 94 percent black and low-achieving, and its staff was mostly white and resided outside the neighborhood. As president of my neighborhood association, the Eastown Community Association (ECA), in 1979 I approached the Sigsbee principal with a proposal to form a committee of representatives from Sigsbee parents, educators, and ECA to solve perceived problems centered on Sigsbee. Although a group was formed and three meetings were held, no common purpose developed. Parents blamed teachers, teachers blamed children and by implication parents, and both groups viewed ECA's interest with suspicion. An all-school parent meeting to discuss school discipline codes was scheduled for the time of the annual open house. It attracted 70 parents, a good turnout generated by ECA's organizers who knocked on doors and passed out flyers in the neighborhood; but the meeting led only to parents' deciding to request of the central office a playground fence, which was soon installed. No further meetings occurred, either by the smaller group or of the larger body.

The lesson of this failure to generate longer-term linkage between community and school lies in the lack of linkage between ECA and parents. ECA, a predominantly white middle-class organization (though it had always had some working-class or minority leaders and organizers), had no direct investment in Sigsbee. That is, its leaders were not settled residents with children at Sigsbee. Sigsbee parents, on the other hand, saw as their principal reference groups the PTA, block clubs, or churches, not ECA. Individual interests never overlapped enough to form a common interest. Goal consensus implies, therefore, shared interests as well as a mechanism to share them.

DETERMINANTS OF NEIGHBORHOOD POLITICAL STYLE WITH RESPECT TO SCHOOL

The case studies thus far presented in this chapter have concerned neighborhoods that already have organizations or at least a group of parents acting collectively on school issues. What factors about neighborhoods and their schools allow some to organize successfully and others not? Harry Summerfield (1971) studied four different neighborhoods in a large city (over one million metropolitan population) in order to answer this question. All names given were fictitious.

The Neighborhoods

King. The first neighborhood, King, was predominantly black and very poor; estimates of its children receiving welfare ranged as high as 85 percent. The principal of the King Elementary School, Mr. Gold, exerted dynamic leadership, both by constant contact with black community leaders in its 95 agencies and organizations and by regular petition of central office officials for more resources for his school. His efforts led to the building of a new air-conditioned school that incorporated under the same roof a neighborhood house, which was a social service agency serving the school's parents and children. He also attracted a disproportionately high share of Title I funds for compensatory education programs and managed to lower the teacher-pupil ratio to 1:23, the lowest of the four schools studied. Faculty morale was high and turnover low. Mr. Gold encouraged every educational innovation he could, preferring to experiment rather than despair over his children's intractably low achievement scores. Active parent involvement, however, was virtually nonexistent; half a dozen was a typical turnout for a PTA meeting. Most parents, though, seemed quietly supportive of Mr. Gold's efforts.

Lawrence. This was an equally poor white enclave. It differed from King, however, in that it resisted political organization. Few residents seemed to care at all about the destiny of the place. For example, when a few of the working-class homeowners tried to organize a regional action committee to advocate for property upkeep, neither tenants nor absentee landlords supported them. Most houses were so deteriorated that the expense of rehabilitating them would either cause losses for the landlords or higher rents for the tenants. When another neighborhood leader sought to organize the Lawrence Residents' Association in order to appeal to agencies after gathering information, he was pleased at the large turnout at the initial meeting, only to discover to his dismay that the residents had come out suspicious of his agenda. Few ultimately supported him.

Lawrence School's principal was the opposite of King's Mr. Gold. He presented himself as passive, if not mildly hostile, toward the community and refused to petition central authorities for more than the minimal resources for his school. As a result, he got few resources and little community support. His pupils' achievement scores were in the lowest decile, and his teachers were unhappy.

Truman. The other two schools were in middle-class areas of the city. Truman School anchored a racially changing neighborhood, mostly white and middle-class, with some black professionals and a growing number of low-income blacks. Conflict in this neighborhood centered on residents' concern over the diminishing quality of education in the school, but they lacked consensus on what to do about it.

Demands never went beyond the neighborhood's boundaries, either from the principal or the parents, to the central authorities. The principal gave only increasingly unsatisfactory verbal reassurances. He was stalemated by lack of direction from the parents and became the focus of resident anxiety.

Larsen. Larsen School was in a white "stable" middle-class neighborhood. Parents, knowledgeable about the school and satisfied with its performance, made no demands on the school itself. They did see themselves as relatively deprived, however, taxed highly but not receiving their fair share in return, especially in the form of a school swimming pool. Concern over this issue and anticipation of possible busing led a group of parents to go directly to the central authorities to demand input into policy decisions. They achieved success.

The Political Styles

Each of the neighborhoods, acting as interest groups with regard to public education, showed different political styles. The King neighborhood demonstrated that if the principal makes demands upon the central authorities, and if those demands are supported by a broad network of neighborhood leadership, the school can receive considerable resources. Larsen neighborhood residents went directly to the central authorities with their concerns and got results, primarily because they acted in unison. Lawrence neighborhood, with neither an activist principal nor an organized resident body, demanded nothing and received as much from central office.

Truman neighbors, though concerned, were divided two ways. The recently arrived low-income blacks, seeing the school as better than what they had experienced before, were complacent. Middle-income whites and blacks denied in effect that the social transition occurring in their neighborhood was affecting their school. The demand they placed on the school was to remain unchanged in spite of changing enrollment. Neighborhood organizing (The Truman Neighborhood Organization) did not deal with the school directly, seeking instead to stabilize the housing patterns of the area. The PTA was concerned with getting rid of unsightly portable classrooms and with quality of education, that is, lessons being aimed at the mediocre student. But neither group dealt with the central office nor did they conflict with the school itself, being alternately content and dissatisfied with the principal's symbolic reassurances. This confusion over goals (should the school adapt or not?) rendered them politically impotent, even though several dozen parents would be classified as active: coming to meetings, voicing opinions, and working on committees.

The Determinants

Summerfield suggested three determinants of these different neighborhood political styles: the function of the principal, how residents manifested deference to school, and whether neighborhood expectations for the school matched available resources.

The function of the principal. "The principal's chief function," he wrote, "is to minimize conflict between the community and the neighborhood school" (1971, p. 93). This statement says nothing about conflict between neighborhood and central officials, however. The successful principal will adopt a style that fits the context. King's Mr. Gold was a dynamic advocate, at once demanding and generating support for his demands among his constituency. This approach did, in fact, reduce conflict between his school and its parents even though most of his students were achieving poorly. The other three principals also saw their roles as reducing conflict, but they did not have to work very hard at doing so because there was little to begin with.

Residents' manifestation of deference for the school. In general the American public is and has been deferential toward education, which accounts for the vast scope and influence of the contemporary education establishment. The public sees education as important to its own well-being and thus supports it. The respect given to educators, however, varies in the ways it is shown. King residents (though many were not active) gave deference in return for community input into policymaking and for the obvious hard work of the school staff. Lawrence neighbors, on the other hand, fearing change that might threaten their survival, gave a deference grounded in ignorance of their own educational needs and in apparent satisfaction with minimal school performance. Truman parents and other citizens also seemed to base their deference on a kind of ignorance: a denial of the effects of social change on their school. The Larsen community's adults supported their school because they knew it was good. Their knowledge came from their involvement with several child-oriented school activities.

Matching resources with expectations. Several points can be made here. To achieve an important new policy or change in the way resources are allocated, neighborhood-based petitioners, Summerfield suggests, must focus on the central authorities, not on the neighborhood principal. Only at this much higher level can such changes occur. The principal can be a valuable ally or advocate, however, and should not be precipitously bypassed. Interest groups can exist in a dormant stage, which may either indicate satisfaction with the status quo or political impotency. Whether there is quiet support of the status quo or overt approval of efforts of elite leaders to create change, this support can be a powerful political act. An elite may be one citizen leader (such as the Lawrence homeowner), an intense, small group (the Truman PTA executive board, for example), chosen representatives (Larsen PTA president), or paid public officials (such as Mr. Gold). An elite seeking change but confused or unsupported will achieve little political strength.

In addition, the feasibility of the changes depends on both the petitioners' goals and the availability of resources. Funds, personnel, building, instructional materials are within the power of school systems to give, states Summerfield, but learning ironically is not. "In many neighborhoods," he writes, "particularly those with extreme educational problems, matching expectations with resources can come to border on the impossible" (1971, p. 97). More specifically, he means, "in the contemporary state of pedagogy, 'learning' is not a commodity politically allocable to great numbers of people of the lower classes." Though technically the statement is correct that learning is not a commodity to be allocated, there is a profound pessimism, if not cynicism, in judging that the poor cannot learn. His point is useful only in reminding organizers that demands should be tangible, such as policy changes, personnel changes, or physical materials or resources, rather than focus on the intangible of learning, spuriously quantified by test scores (but if there is no improvement in scores over time, the organization should begin to question what the educators are doing or not doing, demanding perhaps an outside evaluation).

The final point under this third determinant is that, although many critics of schools hold that the bureaucracies are insulated from the public and closed to their input, Summerfield argues that they are open because neighborhood groups can engage them and make their demands known. Although they cannot make the decision-makers do their will, this fact does not preclude openness. As in all institutions, officials will forestall decisions, compromise, or reach decisions when the timing is right. But Summerfield reminds us of a great obstacle:

"The urban system lacks the money and technology to act on many of its most severe problems" (1971, p. 102). The solution implied is to go beyond, to higher levels of government. Where this lack is actually the case, most mature neighborhood activists have done this in addition to their local efforts.

CONCLUSIONS

What do these and other cases tell us is necessary for successfully organizing linkages between school and neighborhood organization?

1. School conditions that breed low achievement should be carefully documented.
2. Parent feelings of concern for their children's education will fuel the organizing thrust, but these raw emotions need to be informed and appropriate strategies planned to keep the pressure for change constant.
3. Tangible changes, ranging from new instructional materials to personnel transfers, should focus demands. A related, tangible but longer-range and more positive thrust to personnel improvement is to be ever on the lookout for good teachers, to attract them to the school, and to reward in simple ways the ones who are already there. One tangible demand that should always be present is the creation of an official vehicle that will enable parents and other citizens to have policy input. Recall Joyce's concept of responsible parties, mentioned in Chapter 4 (Joyce, Hersh, & McKibbin, 1983).
4. The few cases of successful linkage occurred where only one or two schools were involved. Severe logistical constraints may come into play beyond this limit.
5. Whatever organizing goals are set, they must enjoy reasonably widespread support in the neighborhood. The leadership elite must at least not proceed contrary to the wishes of parents and other residents. A neighborhood organization is in an excellent position to gauge resident opinion through its contacts with various sectors of the neighborhood, including social service agencies.
6. The BUILD Project's success in Buffalo reminds organizers to strive for even broader political support. In Buffalo, the school board was actively involved in planning changes, and the superintendent retained final control, although neither ever exercised their veto power.

7. The neighborhood organization and the parents' group need each other. The organization will never deal meaningfully with school issues without the parents' real investment of their children. The parents, as we saw in Chapter 7, need the broader-based organization to carry their concerns over the longer term. The Eastown Community Association experiment, mentioned earlier, underscores the need for strong ties between the two.

8. Parent education, defined as the development of informed consensus among parents about the purposes of the schools, is a foremost function of organizing. Unfortunately, "parent education" to many educators is a condescending concept that implies the parents have to be taught how to do their job to get their children "ready" for the school experience. In inner-city schools this condescension is too often expressed as ultimate hopelessness: "These people *can't* get them ready." Organizers and good teachers know, on the contrary, that while there are parents in low-income neighborhoods who cannot cope with rearing children because they can scarcely cope with life itself, there are many others who, through collective action, can be "educated" about how their children could best profit from school.

Informed consensus on the purposes of school implies regular information dissemination in order to build agreement on goals. This information should accurately portray what the school is and what it can be.

Thus the goals of organizing for urban school reform are twofold. Neighborhood organizing should promote change in the school as a result of documentation and the application of collective political pressure, and it should build among parents agreement on what their school should do for their children. Both goals require the establishment of a linking mechanism that involves the parents and other residents, at least representationally, in policy decisions at the building level. The next chapter discusses strategies for attaining these goals.

10

Mounting the Campaign to Improve the Neighborhood School

Schools teach those they think they must and when they think they needn't, they don't . . . . There never has been a time in the life of the American public school when we have not known all we needed in order to teach all those whom we chose to teach. (Edmonds, 1985)

The problem of the urban school's failure to educate children at risk is not primarily a technical one; it is a political one. It is a failure of will, not just the will of teachers, administrators, and other system members, but of the broader American society. The neighborhood organization is a political instrument whereby residents can make their educational and other public needs known and have them answered. But it cannot address society at large; it must address school people directly.

What galvanizes parents and other citizens to take action to change their school? Often a school can be highly dysfunctional for its charges, yet parent anger, though widespread, just simmers, never erupting into group action. The lesson from history seems to be that there is usually a precipitating incident or decision that spurs sudden outrage. Typical examples might be closing a neighborhood school, shifting popular personnel, publishing achievement scores by school, or race-based decisions, such as court-ordered busing.

Organizing around these issues has tended to be ad hoc rather than long-term, partially because neighborhood organizations have rarely been involved, but also because of the gulf between professionals and neighborhood people. In addition, parents may not have understood how to mount a campaign to improve their school. Their anxiety has burst into confrontation only when they could see a clear injustice. Poor teaching and poorly operated schools are not clear

148

injustices in the sense that parents and other noneducators have known what the schools should be doing. It is only when parents have a clear understanding of a school's positive goals and operations that they can effectively demand change.

This chapter draws together themes from the school issues discussed in earlier chapters to help neighborhood organizations plan and execute their agendas to improve their neighborhood schools. The first activity must be gathering information on the school while at the same time building consensus among parents and other citizens on what the school should be doing for their children. This planning phase precedes organizational action; however, as the organization encounters obstacles, strategizing will have to shift to overcome them. The chapter closes with vignettes of an effective public school, which the organization should never lose sight of as one of two ultimate goals, the other of which is the inclusion of citizens in the policymaking process of the school.

PLANNING

Building Consensus in the Citizen Group

At the outset, the group should know that most of the educators blame the neighborhood community for the schoolchildren's lack of learning. No matter how the failure is couched, however, there are inner-city school programs that have dealt successfully with it. Is the failure said to be due to truancy? Outreach programs have drastically reduced truancy where they have been built on community support. Is the problem proclaimed to be lack of parental support for children's academic achievement? Success stories of improvement in inner-city children's achievement scores focus on either improved educational method and curriculum or deliberate attempts to involve parents meaningfully in school matters or both. Do educators point the finger at unruly youth in their schools? The school can be made secure through concerted effort, no matter how dangerous the neighborhood. The evidence is there.

The principal organizational goal, therefore, is to create a "can do" attitude in both educators and citizens alike, which will lead to institutionalizing a working relationship. Each group needs the other to achieve the effective school. Citizens will not replace professionals in the implementation of the curriculum, but they can monitor and evaluate many aspects of it. They can also form a political force to attract resources, to change outmoded or harmful policies (even at the district or state levels), and to improve the overall climate of the school.

What are some objectives on which the citizen group could agree regarding the school program? Proficiency in Standard English, in mathematics, and in other content areas such as natural and social science seem as uncontroversial as motherhood. Affective goals, such as student feelings of security, liking for school, and achievement motivation, are goals to be attained by the parents as well. The measurement of these objectives and, even more, the methods by which they are attained are likely to produce controversy, but concensus among residents and between them and educators can be built if all adhere to the "can do" spirit of compromise, especially on the part of educators. Of course, building a spirit of trust in an atmosphere of mistrust and alienation may seem like trying to grow flowers in asphalt, but if the neighborhood organization approaches the school with appropriate third-party support, good information, and components of their plan that will obviously help educators, it stands a chance of winning this spirit of cooperation.

Some other goals the neighborhood organization should strive for are professional autonomy and respect for the teachers by all actors in the school and training programs and other activities for parents and other citizens where need shows. Further specific objectives may have to do with decreasing truancy, overcoming peer pressure against student academic achievement, teacher over- or underreaction to student cultural differences based on culture shock and subsequent lowered expectations of their students, equitable discipline policy fairly administered, appropriate homework, report cards, and parent conference policies.

A final note on goals is needed in this section on building group consensus. Goal displacement is an ever-present threat. Sliding into a "you do it for us" mentality or focusing too narrowly on which parents might get jobs in new programs can quickly destroy the organizing effort.

Observing and Gathering School Data

Parents and other neighborhood citizens can begin to engage the school by observing and documenting how teachers treat students and how the school treats both parents and teachers.[1] Parents have a right to visit their children's classrooms, although many inner-city schools discourage it. Once there, however, observers should become the "fly on the wall," quiet but perceptive, unobtrusively taking notes, saving questions until the appropriate times when teachers, students and personnel are free to talk to them. The more frequently the observers can visit the school the better, so that students and personnel will become accustomed to them and act as they ordinarily do. For working parents this time may be extremely difficult to squeeze in. It might, however, be possible to send older brothers or sisters, grandparents, or other relatives to gather information. The neighborhood organization should provide some brief training in observational techniques, given perhaps by a faculty member of a nearby teacher training institution, to ensure some consistency in reporting.

Categories for observation of teachers include evidence on their attitudes toward students, types of instructional methods and homework policy, and handling of disruptive students. A second group of observational categories concerns administrators' view of teachers: expectations of teachers, teachers' role in school policy, their degree of autonomy, supportive working conditions, professional growth opportunities, and the manner in which they are evaluated.

Teacher behaviors toward students show either high or low expectations of them. For example, neighborhood organization representatives should ask the teacher what the students should be getting out of school. Does the teacher answer that the children should find satisfaction in learning and getting along with others, or merely that they should learn to obey rules? Do the teachers envision students in future positions of employment that require increasing independence and responsibility or do they foresee periodic unemployment and minimal economic security for them?

Do the teacher's instructional activities emphasize discussion skills and reasoning, or mere rote memorization of otherwise unrelated materials? Do teachers give homework that requires students to review classwork, or do they explain that they give no homework because their students are so poor that they have neither privacy nor pencils to do it? If they give homework, do they check it over and return it to the students? How do the teachers help students who are falling behind? Teachers with high expectations will describe how they try to meet the individual needs of each student, and experiment until they find the right approach. Only as a last resort will they refer children to specialists. Teachers with low expectations will reply that they routinely refer these students to special education programs.

What does the teacher do about disruptive students? Better teachers deal with these problems as they arise, first talking privately with the student and suggesting more appropriate ways of acting. Poor disciplinarians respond in extreme ways; they first ignore the behavior, then shout at the student or send the student to the principal. They may also use learning activities, such as looking up words in a dictionary, as punishment for bad behavior. In class discussions, do teachers give equal opportunity to each student to respond, or do they discuss with only a select few? Do they give regular feedback to each student, with positive comments much more frequent than negative ones?

Regarding administrative policy, school administrators can also hold high or low expectations of teachers. School policies can give evidence of their attitude toward teachers. For example, in effective schools, teachers are regularly consulted about new curricula and are involved in textbook selection. They are given regular times for planning, which are not to be used for nonteaching duties such as hall patrol or cafeteria supervision. In short, if they are to function as competent professionals, they must be treated as such. Does school policy encourage professional growth by giving new teachers opportunities to observe and work with more experienced teachers in their classrooms? Are teachers rewarded for becoming familiar with community issues and for using the community as a teaching resource, or are they isolated from community issues?

Evaluations of teachers must focus on how well students are learning. Too often these evaluations merely report on superficial student conformity, based at best on a single observation. Teachers may be rewarded for simply keeping the disciplinary lid on and reprimanded for experimenting with new techniques. Parents and citizens investigating the school must remember that their goal is to improve the process of teacher evaluation, one that helps each teacher improve. The parents themselves should not evaluate the teachers.

Goals and Data Gathering for Change Beyond the Local School

Data should be gathered at the district and state level as well as at the school building itself. Both have considerable impact on the local school. Local neighborhood organizations, particularly if they act in coalition, can make demands on these hierarchies that could go far toward improving local public schools.[2]

At both the state and district levels citizen groups should look at the following practices. What state departments of public instruction and local school districts do about them has direct bearing on the neighborhood school.

Regarding discipline, what are state and district figures on the dropout and suspension rates? When the dropout rate reaches

6 percent or the suspension rate reaches 9 percent, the state must require the district to take corrective action (*All We Need to Know: Educating All of Michigan's Children*, 1985, pp. 8-9). Chemical dependency and truancy must not be handled as disciplinary matters; these problems require a combination of preventive and supportive measures. Corporal punishment should be abolished.[3] A statewide task force on the condition of children at risk, which includes members of the general public, should be created to monitor these conditions.

Regarding tracking and referral, what are the data on ethnic and gender composition at different (assumed) ability levels, and how can students move from low tracks to mainstream or accelerated tracks? Despite some research evidence that homogeneous student groupings succeed within classrooms when they are taught through appropriate methods by enthusiastic teachers, tracking (at the district level) and ability grouping (whole classes within the school) have functioned largely to oppress children at risk (Ornstein & Levine, 1985). For this reason, priority should go to developing and supporting curriculum models that use heterogeneous grouping. A practice related to ability grouping is school counselors' disproportionate referral of students at risk to vocational programs and away from mainstream academic programs. What access do vocational students have to these mainstream programs?

In addition, there has been an increasing tendency for disproportionate referral of children at risk to certain special educational categories, especially "educable mentally retarded," "emotionally impaired," and "learning disabled." Referrals in all other categories have declined in numbers during this same period nationally. If this practice is a new form of disciplinary practice, it must be attacked. Where it reflects need, do special education services have sufficient staff, budget, and authority to assure that these services are delivered properly?

Academic requirements and educational assessment have also been used to push children at risk into lower-track programs or even out of school altogether. Does any proposed increase in graduation requirements or curriculum revision demonstrate in advance how this inequity will not be perpetuated? Furthermore, are the curriculum requirements in compensatory education programs oriented toward helping students quickly and successfully to reenter mainstream courses?

Mention of compensatory education raises the issue of equitable school finance. Data on this are the most difficult of all to obtain, but may also be the most enlightening. What are the per-pupil expenditures across districts and within the district? Are compensatory funds used to supplement district funds at high-need inner-city schools—as they are intended to—or are they used in place of district financing? Obtaining such information may require legal action. Another important objective, particularly at the state level, that citizens should aim for is the provision of financial incentives to local districts to encourage them to work at keeping students in school; to develop programs for preschoolers, pregnant teens, and school-aged parents; and to monitor Title IX requirements. The state should also monitor how districts meet needs of language minorities, requiring bilingual and multicultural programs where appropriate.

ORGANIZING

In the best schools, inner-city or not, an outstanding principal has patiently shaped a quality faculty, and a cohesive community works closely with the principal. The central office, the school board, and the teachers' union are either supportive or at least not obstructive. Folded into the mix of support should be the necessary third-party actors: legal specialists, mental health professionals, independent educational experts (perhaps from a nearby university), politicians, business leaders, union heads, and others.

The neighborhood organization can develop community support through its information-gathering and networking activities (newsletters, meetings, phone chains). The principal as a key figure can influence teacher behavior throughout the school, primarily by working to replace recalcitrant or incompetent teachers with competent ones and by supporting those competent teachers already there. The principal is also the chief procurer of resources from the central office and the board. The best principals know where the good teachers in the school system are and persuade them to join the faculty of the school when the inevitable turnover occurs. They know as well how to get what they need for their school from the main office. They are politically sophisticated and good at keeping their staffs productive and satisfied with their working conditions. The neighborhood organization, in doing its homework, should evaluate the local principal and decide whether it can work with that person or should advocate his or her replacement. If the organization seeks a new principal, it should demand involvement in the selection process.

While waiting for the desired leader to appear, however, the organization must attend to specific changes that information gathering has highlighted. A group called the National Coalition of Advocates for Students (Parents' Guide, 1986, p. 21) has developed guidelines for citizen groups that wish to use information on their local public schools. They suggest a six-step method:

1. Summarize the findings.
2. Consider how to present the findings in a meaningful way. Dissemination might be in a private or a public meeting, a letter, or a report card on school expectations.
3. List the problem areas discovered in order of importance to the students' progress in school.
4. Share the findings.
5. Use the findings to begin a dialogue with all groups interested in school change.
6. When the group gets a win, it should let everyone know about it.

Figures 10.1 and 10.2 list sample grievances and demands.

A major principle to keep in mind is that the group's chances of success increase if it takes on one suggested win at a time. Following this dictum, I will outline tactics on several typical issues that might surface as top priority among the parent/citizen group. This list is not meant to be exhaustive.

Discipline

Parents can be organized on the issue of security and discipline because all parties, including staff and students, understand it and want it. It is a main bridge between the expert and the nonexpert aspects of schooling. Yet there are still obstacles to parent involvement here, because school officials and teachers are loath to acknowledge publicly that they do not have their school under complete control. As with all other school issues, careful documentation will be necessary. The parent/citizen group should not necessarily tell the educators how to discipline but should demand discipline while offering to help in whatever ways they can. Patrols and sentry duty, if required, are not simple jobs and should be undertaken only by trained employees, but some parents could be hired for such roles. Classroom discipline problems can be clarified by parent monitors. Often teachers with an unusual number of disrupters may be doing or not doing something that leads to outbursts or other annoying behavior. Student misbehavior is not always the teacher's fault, of course, but it should not be assumed that it is always the students' fault.

FIGURE 10.1

SAMPLE LIST OF GRIEVANCES

We, the parents of PS ____ demand that our children get a decent education. They cannot get educated under the conditions that are permitted in our school. Here are some of the intolerable things going on right now:

1. Too many good teachers are allowed to leave each year and no one cares.
2. Last week the principal dragged a crying small child by the ear down the hall into his office.
3. Garbage is constantly left uncovered in the hallways. We have many roaches, waterbugs, and rats.
4. The principal is unavailable to the parents. If any of us do get in to see him he is always evasive and uncommunicative.
5. The principal refused to make reading scores available to the parents.
6. When one fourth-grade teacher sent a child to the office to be reprimanded, the principal pushed the child away, saying, "I don't want to be bothered."
7. Children who have trouble reading are not given adequate help.
8. The principal shouts at teachers in front of the children.
9. The principal refuses to permit any teacher assistants from our community in his school.
10. The principal failed to attend sixth-grade Arista Assembly.
11. The principal plays black and Puerto Rican parents against each other.
12. The principal has set up no supervision of the playground during lunch period.
13. The principal allows the teachers to park their cars in the playground.
14. Two third-grade classes were refused lunch as punishment for misbehavior. When parents complained, the principal just shrugged.
15. The principal gives a biased description of children to new teachers.
16. Children are permitted to fight in halls with teachers ignoring them.

Source: Lurie, E. (1970). *How to change the schools: A parents' action handbook on how to fight the system* (pp. 152-53). New York: Vintage. Reprinted with permission.

Suspension of a student is a drastic disciplinary practice in any school. There are particular difficulties with it in an inner-city school (Lurie, 1970, pp. 198–204). In addition, school officials often ignore regulations regarding suspension, holding hearings, for example, where the principal is both arresting officer and judge.[4] Rules are often inconsistent and secret; sometimes suspensions are simply the result of

FIGURE 10.2

SAMPLE LIST OF DEMANDS

We the undersigned demand that immediate steps be taken to
correct conditions at JHS___. We further demand that the
principal be replaced with someone more attuned to the needs
of our children. We are willing to meet and discuss any
point in our demands, except the removal of Mr. ___. We give
the local school board and the Board of Education the balance
of the school year and the summer recess to make necessary
changes. We want:

1. A more available and capable principal.
2. More reading teachers.
3. Control of teacher absenteeism. If a teacher must be
   absent, arrangements must be made so that the same
   substitute goes to a class each time.
4. We demand that a committee of parents and teachers be
   immediately set up to develop standards for teaching.
   All teachers who can't or won't conform to these
   standards should be replaced.
5. Our children should be considered just "children"
   without any disparaging adjectives.
6. An exterminator must come to our school regularly
   until the roaches and rats are gone. Garbage should
   covered and put away properly.
7. Fifteen teacher assistants to be immediately assigned
   to our school for thirty hours a week each.
8. The reading scores for our school must be made public
   at once and a program for improving the reading of the
   children worked out by the teachers and supervisors.
9. In addition to removing the principal, Mr. ___ and
   Mrs. ___ must be immediately removed from our teaching
   staff. We will not prejudice their future employment
   elsewhere by stating our reasons here.
10. The following twelve teachers must be required to take
    a sensitivity course and a teaching-skills course this
    summer if they are to remain in our school. (Names
    follow.) Failing this, grant them transfers to schools
    more suitable to their talents.
11. Parents should be made welcome in this school by
    principal and staff.
12. Necessary repairs be immediately attended to in the
    library, lunchroom, and gym.
13. That a written reaction to these demands be received
    before our next general parent meeting in May. This
    must be sent to us no later than ___.

Source: Lurie, E. (1970). *How to change the schools: A
parents' action handbook on how to fight the system* (pp. 153-
54). New York: Vintage. Reprinted with permission.

political disagreements between students and authorities (for example, putting up a Malcolm X poster). Although suspension is supposed to help children, it almost always harms them, especially when used to push students out of school. Finally, school boards may keep totally inadequate records on suspensions.

However the issue of discipline, including suspension, in the school is framed, it should lead to the goal of regular discussions between parent/citizen groups and staff. As much attention should be paid to positive reinforcements for good behavior as to punishment for bad. At the high-school level, even possibly at the middle-school level, students should be involved in setting discipline policy. Veteran inner-city principals have formed "war councils" of gang leaders in their student body to head off impending gang violence (Greenstein, 1985). Involving students in school operation is such an important source of positive reinforcement that I will discuss it in a separate section below.

Teacher Evaluation

At some point in the linking process between school and neighborhood, perhaps even at the outset, teacher evaluation will become the issue. Ellen Lurie (1970), a veteran New York City parent activist, suggested being very practical in the how-to-do-it phase once the group has decided to gather data on teacher performance. Who will help do the evaluation? she asks. When? How often? Will the group give teachers advance notice of visitation or not? Will it be by formal questionnaire or informally? Will the evaluation include the teachers' attitudes toward the community? Will the school evaluation include evidence of administrators' attitudes toward teachers and parents? How will the findings be used?

> Will you discuss your findings directly with the teachers involved? Will you submit them to the principal? To the local school board? Will you make your findings public? (p. 4)

Lurie also suggests investigating local teacher-training institutions that supply teachers for the schools, as well as examining training procedures for paraprofessionals.

Lurie's militancy grew out of heated battles with the bureaucrats of New York City's public school system. With hindsight, she thinks that parents should demand of the school board that they involve parents in establishing a procedure for evaluating staff performance in the district. Most districts already have teacher evaluation procedures, of course, but few involve noneducators, since the ethic of professionalism by definition excludes laymen. If the board drags its feet, she asserts, parents still have a right to set up their own committee and develop criteria for evaluating their own school's staff.

Let the neighborhood organizers be aware, however, that this issue is explosive. It is probably wise to postpone it until much later in the organizing campaign. Demands in this area run a considerable risk of polarizing the parties, no matter when they are made. When they are presented first, they are tantamount to a declaration of war from the perspective of the teachers' union. The issue may ultimately be more winnable if it is couched in terms of assisting a supportive principal in the evaluation of teachers.

Homework

Another issue that can irritate conscientious parents is homework, because the amount and quality of homework given varies widely across schools. Schools with high expectations for students sometimes go to excess, loading them down with three or more hours of work per night, creating tension in the family when some of the work cannot be done by the child alone, who comes pleading to the parents for help. Other schools, particularly inner-city schools, give none at all, protesting that the children have no quiet place at home in which to work or that they have few books at home.

Whether or not homework is more beneficial to low achievers than to high achievers, as some studies claim, it does appear useful to all when it is carefully monitored and given back to each child. If the teacher does this aspect of the instructional job carefully and conscientiously, the issues of amount and quality may well take care of themselves. Some schools set up an after-school homework period for all children, which includes, of course, those who actually have no quiet space at home in which to work.

Parent-Teacher Conferences

Often too brief and with little privacy, these meetings can find parents given doubletalk, lectured, or asked embarrassing questions. For example, if the parents ask how their child is doing in reading, they might be told he is doing fine—which means that he is behaving himself quietly. If an aggressive parent asks to see the evidence, the parent might be told that such scores are confidential (the experience of Lurie in 1970 in New York). At the very least, the teacher should be clear in his or her statements about the child and should explain all data without having to be asked. Teachers should not ask probing questions unless they are relevant. If at all possible, conference times should be at the convenience of the parents because the place is at the convenience of the teacher. Reasonable time and privacy should also be given. Parents should be welcome at the school.

Report Cards

Report cards represent a problem of equity because standards may vary widely from teacher to teacher and from school to school (Lurie, 1970). Many inner-city teachers, underestimating the intelligence of their students, will grade them either too low or artificially high. The latter situation is an attempt to avoid recriminations by either students or parents, for if students lose faith entirely, goes the rationale, they may be impossible to control (Ornstein & Levine, 1985). Teachers sometimes punish students for undesirable behavior by lowering their acadmic grade. They may also increase an academic grade for equally irrelevant reasons, such as nice clothing or handsome appearance.

Even if report-card grades were more accurate, however, they would retain some drawbacks. They heighten competition between children, drawing their focus to studying for marks alone. Students who get unfair grades may have no way to appeal them. Report cards can often mystify parents rather than inform them when the marks are not explained.

If parents wish to retain report cards, they should see to it that they are consistent across teachers and even schools, that the marks reflect the child's academic achievement, and that the system of reporting be made clear to all parents. Setting up a process for appealing grades might also be a good issue for discussion.

Student Participation in School Operations

Easy to overlook as the neighborhood organization seeks greater influence in the local school is the need for the students themselves to become invested in their own school by participating in its life. The following ways of doing so assume that students are high-school aged, but the principles of student participation as a main source of positive reinforcement extend down through the elementary school. Students at the appropriate age levels should be able

1. To elect their own student government and spend their own funds
2. To publish their own newspaper without prior censorship
3. To hold meetings in school without the presence of staff
4. To participate in screening, hiring, evaluating, and dismissing teachers
5. To review curriculum requirements and participate in setting standards and selecting textbooks
6. To dress as they wish
7. To establish and maintain rules concerning attendance and discipline
8. To criticize school authorities and policies without fear of repression or punishment

Many parents and staff in high schools would look upon these rights with horror. Nonetheless, if parents wish to participate significantly in the school process, they cannot deny that wish to their children. It would be political suicide for the two weakest groups to split over this matter of who will participate.

We have now discussed briefly some of the major problem areas that the neighborhood organization must deal with in its school improvement campaign. Focusing exclusively on problems, however, can distract from the vision of what the school can become. It is useful, therefore, for the laborers in this long-term struggle to remind themselves of what it is they are struggling for: the successful school. Here is a summary of its characteristics.

THE SUCCESSFUL INNER-CITY PUBLIC SCHOOL

"Success" includes two meanings. In the minimalist sense, the successful school enables the vast majority of its students, at least 85 to 90 percent, to achieve at grade level or above in reading and computation. The more comprehensive sense of positive, even exciting, school climate includes security, support of student academic achievement, and promotion of a sense of community among staff, students, and parents.

Consider the successful elementary school. Although the neighborhood may be poor, dreary, and crime-ridden, the school staff has adapted to the shortcomings these conditions may produce in the children's capacity to succeed in school. The principal knows all the children by name and visits their families at home once a year. The teachers know their own students and also visit them. Although they may not live in the neighborhood, they know it reasonably well and are aware of its strengths as well as its weaknesses. The professional staff experiences relatively little turnover because members plan and even socialize together; they enjoy their work, and they are competent.

The school is of manageable size (fewer than 400 students). The building, perhaps quite old, is kept neat and in good condition, as are the grounds. Graffiti inside have been replaced by student works of art and by numerous public commendations of individual students. Every attempt is made to recognize the uniqueness of each student, not only in academic terms but in every other way possible.

For the most part the teachers are experienced in and knowledgeable of the linguistic and cultural differences the students may bring with them to school. They are aware in the early grades that one of their principal functions is to help children read Standard English. To this end, they focus on training the perceptual skills of students who speak black English vernacular to help them hear and make distinctions in Standard English that have no function in their own dialect (Labov, 1972). For instance, they will teach such a child to read "-ed" as a marker of the past tense in Standard English, because "-ed" does not exist in the child's spoken language. The potential for misunderstanding the language of instruction by black English vernacular speakers is also particularly great in mathematics and science.[5]

Instruction in these grades is usually in short lessons so that the teacher can make sure each child understands each step and can provide immediate feedback to that child (Woolfolk & McCune-Nicolich, 1984). Short daily assignments in which students keep records on their own work help build student responsibility. These children are taught problem-solving techniques and how to monitor their own learning, so that they can tell when they are using these techniques correctly. There are never long periods of seatwork; when seatwork is used, it is short and is preceded and followed by teacher presentations and is monitored by the teacher. There is time, however, for plenty of repetition and practice.

Despite all this structure, the classroom atmosphere is friendly and supportive. Teachers handle discipline as positively as possible. They show evidence of careful planning, of communication of rules set down and consistently enforced from the outset, of awareness of what each student is supposed to be doing—and actually is doing—as the group moves through its daily routine. Yet each classroom demonstrates an individual personality, both of its teacher and of its students. There is opportunity to innovate and to respond to particular teacher and student interests. Above all, the teachers like the students and strongly believe all of them can learn.

Effective secondary classrooms and schools share most of these characteristics, although we would expect more lecturing, explaining, and discussing to occur. Lectures would be clear, well organized, but not too long. While speaking, teachers would move about the room, maintaining eye contact with students and occasionally asking questions to keep attention focused. Materials would be at the appropriate level of difficulty for each student, which implies a wide range of materials. To the extent possible the teacher would tailor the lessons to fit the needs of individual students, here giving some an assignment, there giving others a number of choices in their work.

While it might be possible for isolated effective classrooms to exist within an ineffective school, it is highly unlikely. Thus, the long-term goals of the change process must be to make the entire school effective. By now it should be understood that the effective school involves parents and other neighborhood residents at all levels of its operation.

CONCLUSION

Throughout its campaign to improve the local public school, the neighborhood organization must keep before its collective eye above all else the vision of becoming part of the governance of the school in order to ensure that parents' and students' voices will be heard and heeded. The responsible party approach, mentioned in Chapter 4, is the most politically feasible solution because it involves all interested parties. To reiterate the concept, this collaborative school-site governance unit would include representatives from five sectors: the general public, site and district administrators, teachers, technical consultants, and parents and students. This group would have budgetary, personnel, and curriculum powers; but to allay fears at the district level that control would be abused, its decisions could be appealed to the school board and the superintendent and overturned, if necessary. In fact, the guidelines for its operation would be drawn up in consultation with these authorities.

This chapter has highlighted points to consider in conducting a campaign to create a responsible party, but the neighborhood organization leaders should always insist that this group be constituted. It is a common tendency as a school improves in response to community demand for the community group to retreat to a passive stance, leaving the school to run its affairs. This last step of institutionalizing residents into neighborhood educational policymaking is the hardest to take and will encounter perhaps the most resistance, depending on the context of the particular city, but it is the most crucial if long-term change is to be pursued and achieved. It is the only way each school will come to "choose to teach" *all* its students.

Notes

CHAPTER 2

1. See Meyer Weinberg (1983, pp. 55–85). In this chapter on race and IQ, Weinberg not only provides a detailed history of the controversy surrounding racially motivated IQ testing but also demonstrates that no convincing evidence has ever been offered in support of the hypothesis that racial differences in IQ are hereditary. By the end of the 1920s, the vast majority of American genetic scientists were of the same opinion as Weinberg.

2. These themes were verified in January, 1986, in a CBS documentary, *The Vanishing Family: Black America in Crisis.* Bill Moyers interviewed several blacks in Newark, New Jersey, about their attitudes toward the opposite sex, childbearing out of wedlock, and welfare. A panel discussion by four black experts following the presentation indicted the black community's leadership for failing to socialize the youth more effectively. They hinted at, but did not explore fully, the many ways that the larger society is implicated in the problems of the ghetto.

3. Two articles on the EXCEL program, one by Jackson himself and the other raising questions about his approach, can be found in Rich (1985, pp. 54–65).

CHAPTER 3

1. Foster suggests that there are four distinct subgroupings within the low-income population of an inner-city high school. Seventeen percent are middle-class in orientation and behavior. Sixty percent display street-corner behavior but are capable of internalizing middle-class values of hard work and achievement motivation. About 6 percent are religiously or politically militant, and 18 percent have emotional or mental problems that qualify them as disturbed or retarded in some fashion. Foster gives no source for these figures, but they rang true from my experience as a teacher in an all-black working-class big city public high school.

2. This point about misunderstanding each other's behaviors, especially students misinterpreting teacher behavior, has been made by other observers. See, for example, Edward Ladd (1972, pp. 331–47).

3. See Thomas Peters and Robert Waterman (1982, pp. 93–118), for a summary of four stages in the development of management theory.

CHAPTER 4

1. Carl Bereiter (1985), a professor of applied psychology, was an early proponent of the technical approach. He parted company, however, with the IGE model in its assumption that the teacher could diagnose individual differences in students and then structure appropriate learning experiences. He called this assumption "highly questionable," based on our present level of knowledge.

CHAPTER 5

1. However, Paul E. Peterson (1985) provides evidence of substantial support among the working class for the extension of public schooling.

2. Elsewhere I (Williams, 1984) have called this view the administrative model of community organizing.

3. See David Claerbaut (1983), Chapter 2. Other forces, principally the rise of the multinational corporation, also seriously contributed to northern urban decline by providing avenues for the withdrawal of capital and jobs to other countries.

CHAPTER 6

1. Anthony Lukas (1985) details the growth and decline of ROAR and of spin-off groups that defected from it because of its nonviolent stance.

2. Michael Harrington (1984, pp. 65–94), develops this larger figure on the basis of a more liberal understanding of the definition of poverty. The Reagan administration, as of August, 1985, had claimed an "improvement" to "only" 33.7 million poor.

CHAPTER 8

1. According to Philip Cusick's (1983) study of the "entrepreneurial" high school, the teachers were on their own to create interesting courses for students.

2. Recall the discussion of neighborhood leadership types in Chapter 7. Neighborhood radicals and respectable militants would be the most likely to emerge as leaders for school improvement in the inner city.

3. Summerfield (1971) concluded that elites (leaders) who were confused about their goals or who lacked a constituency could generate little or no leverage with school officials.

CHAPTER 9

1. Paul David Wellstone (1978) and William Ellis (1969) both discuss how organizers and leaders in the organizations they studied managed both advocacy and service demands on themselves.

CHAPTER 10

1. Much of this analysis on the next three pages is adapted from *A Parents' Guide* (1986).

2. Most of these goals and objectives are elaborated in *All We Need to Know* (1985).

3. The most comprehensive and compelling argument against corporal punishment that I have seen in print comes from Jack Greenstein (1985, pp. 178–84). Greenstein wrote from his 23 years' experience as a teacher and principal in Chicago's inner-city schools.

4. See William Rioux (1980, pp. 29–33, 43–54), for up-to-date, clear question-and-answer statements on the legal status of suspension and other forms of discipline, including corporal punishment.

5. Eleanor Orr (1987) analyzed how differences in usage, especially of prepositions and conjunctions, between black English vernacular and Standard English lead to students' misinterpretation of the meanings of problems in math and science. Although this understanding is a technical one on the part of Standard English speaking teachers, the time lag between the linguists' work of the 1960s, for example William Labov (1972), and its application to education in the late 1980s is yet another evidence of the lack of political will in white society to solve the persistent problems of educating the disadvantaged of the United States.

References

Ahlbrandt, R. S., & Cunningham, J. V. (1979). *A new public policy for neighborhood preservation.* New York: Praeger.

Alinsky, S. D. (1972a, January). [Interview]. *Playboy.*

Alinsky, S. D. (1972b). *Rules for radicals.* New York: Vintage.

All we need to know: Educating all of Michigan's children. (1985). Ann Arbor, MI: Student Advocacy Center (617 E. University, Ann Arbor MI 48104).

Bailey, R., Jr. (1972). *Radicals in urban politics: The Alinsky approach.* Chicago: University of Chicago Press.

Ballenger, B. (1981). Why people join. *Community Jobs, 5*(3), 3-6.

Bereiter, C. (1985, April). The changing face of educational disadvantagement. *Phi Delta Kappan,* 538-40.

Berger, E. H. (1981). *Parents as partners in education: The school and home working together.* St. Louis, MO: C. V. Mosby.

Berger, P. L., & Neuhaus, R. J. (1977). *To empower people: The role of mediating structures in public policy.* Washington, DC: American Enterprise Institute.

Berube, M. R. (1984). *Education and poverty: Effective schooling in the United States and Cuba.* Westport, CT: Greenwood Press.

Betts, R. (1978). *Acting out: Coping with big city schools.* Boston: Little, Brown.

Borman, K., & Spring, J. (1984). *Schools in central cities: Structure and process.* New York: Longman.

Boyer, E. L. (1983). *High school: A report on secondary education in America.* New York: Harper & Row.

Boyte, H. (1980). *The backyard revolution: Understanding the new citizen movement.* Philadelphia, PA: Temple University Press.

Bradbury, K. L., Downs, A., & Small, K. A. (1982). *Urban decline and the future of American cities.* Washington, DC: The Brookings Institution.

Brown, F. (1978, May). Community control that succeeded. *The Educational Forum,* pp. 451-57.

Bryan, W. L. (1981, March/April). Preventing burnout in the public interest. *The Grantsmanship Center News,* pp. 15-77.

Callahan, R. (1962). *Education and the cult of efficiency.* Chicago: University of Chicago Press.

Cincotta, G. (1986, April 12). [Keynote address to First Neighborhood Convention, Grand Rapids, Michigan.]

Claerbaut, D. (1983). *Urban ministry*. Grand Rapids, MI: Zondervan.

Clark, R. (1983). *Family life and school achievement: Why poor black children succeed or fail*. Chicago: University of Chicago Press.

Comer, J. P. (1980). *School power: Implications of an intervention project*. New York: Free Press.

Coombs, J. R. (1985). Can minimum competency testing be justified? In J. M. Rich (Ed.), *Innovations in education: Reformers and their critics* (pp. 159–166). Boston: Allyn and Bacon.

Cooper, H. M., & Good, T. L. (1983). *Pygmalion grows up: Studies in the expectation communication process*. New York: Longman.

Crowfoot, J., Bryant, B., & Chesler, M. (1982). *Action for educational equity: A guide for parents and members of community groups*. Boston: Institute for Responsive Education.

Cuban, L. (1984). Transforming the frog into a prince: Effective schools research, policy, and practice at the district level. *Harvard Educational Review, 54*(2), 129–151.

Cusick, P. A. (1983). *The egalitarian ideal and the American high school: Studies of three schools*. New York: Longman.

Dahl, R. (1960). The analysis of influence in local communities. In C. R. Adrian (Ed.), *Social science and community action* (pp. 25–42). East Lansing, MI: Michigan State University Press.

Damerell, R. G. (1985). *Education's smoking gun: How teachers colleges have destroyed education in America*. New York: Freundlich Books.

Davies, D. (1981). Citizen participation in decision making in the schools. In D. Davies (Ed.), *Communities and their schools* (pp. 83–119). New York: McGraw-Hill.

Davies, D., et al. (1979) *Patterns of citizen participation in educational decisionmaking* (Vol. II): *Grassroots perspectives: Diverse forms of participation*. Boston: Institute for Responsive Education.

Davis, B., & Arnof, D. (1983). *How to fix what's wrong with our schools*. New Haven, CT: Ticknor and Fields.

Downs, A. (1981). *Neighborhoods and urban development*. Washington, DC: The Brookings Institution.

Edmonds, R. (1983). How can we advocate for effective schools? In *Excellence and equity, quality and inequality: A report on civil rights, education and black children* (pp. 22–24). Washington, DC: National Black Child Development Institute.

Edmonds, R. (1985). [Quoted in frontispiece of *All we need to know: Educating all of Michigan's children*]. Ann Arbor, MI: Student Advocacy Center.

Felt, M. C. (1985). *Improving our schools: Thirty-three studies that inform local action*. Newton, MA: Education Development Center.

Fish, J. H. (1973). *Black power/white control: The struggle of the Woodlawn Organization in Chicago*. Princeton, NJ: Princeton University Press.

Fisher, R. (1984). *Let the people decide: Neighborhood organizing in America*. Boston, MA: Twayne Publishers.

Fogarino, S. (1981). The Community Board Program (CBP): Neighbors helping neighbors. *Community Jobs*, 4(10), 3–5.

Foster, H. L. (1974). *Ribbin', jivin', and playin' the dozens*. Cambridge, MA: Ballinger.

Gittell, M. (1980). *Limits to citizen participation: The decline of community organizations*. Beverly Hills, CA: Sage.

Goetze, R. (1979). *Understanding neighborhood change: The role of expectations in urban revitalization*. Cambridge, MA: Ballinger.

Grace, G. (Ed.). (1984). *Education and the city: Theory, history, and contemporary practice*. London: Routledge and Kegan Paul.

Greenstein, J. (1985). *What the children taught me*. Chicago: University of Chicago Press.

Gross, N. (1958). Local pressures on the public school administration. In G. Bereday & L. Volpicelli (Eds.), *Public education in America: A new interpretation of purpose and practice* (pp. 132–43). New York: Harper and Brothers.

Guthrie, J. W., Kleindorfer G. B., Levin H. M., & Stout, R. T. (1971). *Schools and inequality*. Cambridge, MA: MIT Press.

Hallman, H. W. (1984). *Neighborhoods: Their place in urban life*. Beverly Hills, CA: Sage.

Harrington, M. (1984). *The new American poverty*. New York: Holt, Rinehart, and Winston.

Hatton, B. (1979). Community control in retrospect: A review of strategies for community participation in education. In C. Grant (Ed.), *Community participation in education* (pp. 2–20). Boston: Allyn and Bacon.

Havighurst, R. J. (1979). Local community participation in educational policy making and school administration. In C. Grant (Ed.), *Community participation in education* (pp. 22–24). Boston: Allyn and Bacon.

Howard, J., & Hammond, R. (1985, September 9). Rumors of inferiority. *The New Republic*, pp. 17–21.

James, R. (1973). National Strategies for neighborhood control and citizen participation. In G. Frederickson (Ed.), *Neighborhood control in the 1970s: Politics, administration, and citizen participation* (pp. 179–94). New York: Chandler.

Joyce, B. R., Hersh, R., & McKibbin, M. (1983). *The structure of school improvement*. New York: Longman.

Kahn, S. (1982). *Organizing: A guide for grassroots leaders*. New York: McGraw-Hill.

Karp, W. (1985, June). Why Johnny can't think: The politics of bad schooling. *Harper's*, p. 73.

Katz, D., & Kahn, R. L. (1978). *The social psychology of organizations* (2nd ed.). New York: Wiley.

Katz, M. B. (Ed.) (1973). *Education in American history: Readings on the social issues.* New York: Praeger.

Kettl, D. F. (1981). Blocked out? The plight of the poor in grant reform. *Journal of Community Action, I*(2), 13–18.

Kohl, H. (1984). *Basic skills.* Toronto: Bantam.

Kozol, J. (1967). *Death at an early age: The destruction of the hearts and minds of Negro children in the Boston public schools.* New York: Houghton Mifflin.

Labov, W. (1972). Some sources of reading problems for Negro speakers of nonstandard English. In R. D. Abrahams & R. C. Troike (Eds.), *Language and cultural diversity in American education* (pp. 274–89). Englewood Cliffs, NJ: Prentice-Hall.

Ladd, E. T. (1972). Moving to positive strategies for order-keeping with kids accustomed to restrictions, threats, and punishments. *Urban Education, 6*(4), 331–47.

Lamb, C. (1975). *Political power in poor neighborhoods.* New York: Schenkman.

Lancourt, J. (1979). *Confront or concede: The Alinsky citizen-action organizations.* Lexington, MA: D.C. Heath.

LaNoue, G., & Smith, B. (1971). Decentralization. In *The encyclopedia of education* (Vol. 5). New York: Macmillan.

Lantner, P. (1968). The short, happy life of the Adams Morgan Community School Project. *Harvard Educational Review, 38*(2), 235–62.

Lee, B. A., Oropesa R. S., Metch J. M., Guest A. M. (1984). Testing the decline-of-community thesis: Neighborhood organizations in Seattle, 1929 and 1979. *American Journal of Sociology, 89*(5), 1161–88.

Leff, L. (1981, May 13). Local groups that aid poor flourish by using confrontation tactics. *Wall Street Journal,* pp. 31–55.

Lemann, N. (1986, June, July). The origins of the underclass. *The Atlantic Monthly,* pp. 54–68.

Levin, H. M. (1987). Accelerated schools for disadvantaged students. *Educational Leadership, 44*(6), 19–21.

Lightfoot, S. L. (1983). *The good high school: Portraits of character and culture.* New York: Basic Books.

Litwak, E., & Meyer, H. (1974). *School, Family, and neighborhood: The theory and practice of school-community relations.* New York: Columbia University Press.

Lukas, J. (1985). *Common ground: A turbulent decade in the lives of three American families.* New York: Alfred A. Knopf.

Lurie, E. (1970). *How to change the schools: A parents' action handbook on how to fight the system.* New York: Vintage.

Marciniak, E. (1981). *Reversing urban decline.* Washington, DC: National Center for Urban Ethnic Affairs.

Mayer, N. S. (1984). *Neighborhood organizations and community development: Making revitalization work.* Washington, DC: Urban Institute Press.

Meier, A., & Rudwick, E. (1973). Early boycotts of segregated schools: The case of Springfield, Ohio, 1922–23. In M. Katz (ed.), *Education and American history: Readings on the social issues* (pp. 290–300). New York: Praeger.

Miller, Z. L. (1981). The role and concept of neighborhood in American cities. In R. Fisher & P. Romanofsky (Eds.), *Community organization for urban social change: A historical perspective* (pp. 3–32). Westport, CT: Greenwood Press.

Morris, R. S. (1980). *Bum rap on America's cities: The real causes of urban decay.* Englewood Cliffs, NJ: Prentice-Hall.

Moyers, B. (Director). (1986). *The vanishing family: Black America in crisis* [Film]. New York: CBS News.

Naison, M. (1981). Harlem communists and the politics of black protest. In R. Fisher & P. Romanofsky (Eds.), *Community organization for urban social change: A historical perspective* (pp. 89–126). Westport, CT: Greenwood Press.

National Commission on Educational Excellence. (1983). *A nation at risk: The imperative for educational reform.* Washington, DC: Author.

Nix, H. (1976). Community leadership. In W. Lassey & R. Fernandez (Eds.), *Leadership and social change* (pp. 313–24). LaJolla, CA: University Associates.

Ogbu, J. (1974). *The next generation: An ethnography of education in an urban neighborhood.* New York: Academic Press.

Organizing for family and congregation. (1978). Huntington, NY: Industrial Areas Foundation.

Ornstein, A. C., & Levine, D. U. (1985). *An introduction to the foundations of education* (3rd ed.). Boston: Houghton Mifflin.

Orr, E. W. (1987). *Twice as less: Black English and the performance of black students in mathematics and science.* New York: W. W. Norton.

O'Shea, D. (1975). School district decentralization: The case of Los Angeles. *Education and Urban Society, 7*(4), 377–92.

Owen, S. V., Froman, R. D., & Moscow, H. (1981). *Educational psychology: An introduction* (2nd ed.). Boston: Little, Brown.

Parents' Guide: Measuring Your School's Expectations. (no date). Ann Arbor, MI: Student Advocacy Center (617 E. University, Ann Arbor, MI 48104).

Payne, C. M. (1984). *Getting what we ask for: The ambiguity of success and failure in urban education.* Westport, CT: Greenwood Press.

Perlman, J. E. (1976). Grassrooting the system. *Social Policy, 7,* 4–20.

Peters, T. J., & Waterman, R. H., Jr. (1982). *In search of excellence: Lessons from America's best-run companies.* New York: Harper and Row.

Peterson, P. E. (1985). *The politics of school reform, 1870–1940.* Chicago: University of Chicago Press.

Piven, F. F., & Cloward, R. A. (1977). *Poor people's movements: Why they succeed, how they fail.* New York: Pantheon.

Popkewitz, T. S., Tabachnick, B. R., & Wehlage, G. (1982). *The myth of educational reform: A study of school responses to a program of change.* Madison, WI: University of Wisconsin Press.

Purkey, S. C., & Smith, M. S. (1983). Effective schools: A review. *The Elementary School Journal*, 83(4), 427–53.

Ravitch, D. (1983). *The troubled crusade: American education 1945–1980*. *New York: Basic Books*.

Report of the National Advisory Commission on Civil Disorders. (1968). New York: Bantam Books.

Rich, J. M. (Ed.). (1985). *Innovations in education: Reformers and their critics* (4th ed.). Boston: Allyn and Bacon.

Rich, R. C. (1980). The dynamics of leadership in neighborhood organizations. *Social Science Quarterly*, 60(4), 570–87.

Rioux, W. (1980). *You can improve your child's school*. New York: Simon and Schuster.

Rogers, D., & Chung, N. H. (1983). *110 Livingston Street revisited: Decentralization in action*. New York: New York University Press.

Rosenfeld, G. (1971). *"Shut those thick lips!" A study of slum school failure*. New York: Holt, Rinehart, and Winston.

Rosenthal, R., & Jacobson, L. (1968). *Pygmalion in the classroom: Teacher expectation and pupils' intellectual development*. New York: Holt, Rinehart, and Winston.

Ryan, W. (1971). *Blaming the victim*. New York: Random House.

Sarason, S. B. (1971). *The culture of the school and the problem of change*. Boston: Allyn and Bacon.

Sarason, S. B. (1983). *Schooling in America: Scapegoat and salvation*. New York: Free Press.

Schoenberg, S. P., & Rosenbaum, P. L. (1980). *Neighborhoods that work: Sources for viability in the inner city*. New Brunswick, NJ: Rutgers University Press.

Seeley, D. S. (1981). *Education through partnership: Mediating structures and education*. Cambridge, MA: Ballinger.

Sieber, R. T. (1982). The politics of middle class success in an inner city public school. *Journal of Education*, 164(1), 30–47.

Spring, J. (1972). *Education and the rise of the corporate state*. Boston: Beacon Press.

Summary of the History of Title I: Parent Involvement Highlights. (no date). Washington, DC: National Parent Center (1314 145h St. NW, Suite 6, Washington, D.C. 20005).

Summerfield, H. L. (1971). *The neighborhood-based politics of education*. Columbus, OH: Charles Merrill.

Tofani, L. (1985, November 24). Time hasn't healed bitterness between teacher and town. *Grand Rapids Press*, p. A21.

Tyack, D. (1973). Bureaucracy and the common school: The example of Portland, Oregon, 1851-1913. In Katz, M.D. (Ed.), *Education in American history: Readings on the social issues* (pp. 164–181). New York: Praeger.

Tyack, D. (1981). Governance and goals: Historical perspectives on public education. In Don Davies (Ed.), *Communities and their schools* (pp. 11–31). New York: McGraw-Hill.

Violas, P. (1978). *The training of the urban working class: A history of twentieth century American education.* Chicago: Rand McNally.

Warren, R., & Warren, D. (1977). *The neighborhood organizer's handbook.* Notre Dame, IN: University of Notre Dame Press.

Wayland, S. (1958). The school as community center. In G. Bereday & L. Volpicelli (Eds.), *Public education in America: A new interpretation of purpose and practice* (pp. 161–73). New York: Harper and Brothers.

Webb, R. (1981). *Schooling and society.* New York: Macmillan.

Weinberg, M. (1983). *The search for quality integrated education: Policy and research on minority students in school and college.* Westport, CT: Greenwood Press.

Wellman, B., & Leighton, B. (1979). Networks, neighborhoods, and communities: Approaches to the study of the community question. *Urban Affairs Quarterly, 14*(3), 363–390.

Williams, M. R. (1980, September 13). *The urban school and the neighborhood association: Toward building a working relationship.* Paper presented at AERA Regional Conference on the Social Context of Education. Western Michigan University, Kalamazoo, MI.

Williams, M. R. (1984). Two models of community organizing. *Urban Affairs Quarterly, 19*(4), 568–73.

Williams, M. R. (1985). *Neighborhood organizations: Seeds of a new urban life.* Westport, CT: Greenwood Press.

Winner, L. (1977). *Autonomous technology: Technics-out-of-control as a theme in political thought.* Cambridge, MA: MIT Press.

Woolfolk, A. E., & McCune-Nicolich, L. (1984). *Educational psychology for teachers* (2nd ed.). Englewood Cliffs, NJ: Prentice-Hall.

Index

Adams Morgan School Project, 95
Addams, Jane, 74
Ahlbrandt, R. S., 108
Alinsky, Saul D., 2, 4, 64, 77, 81, 95,
    102-103, 109-110, 112, 114, 123, 137,
    139
*All We Need to Know: Educating All of
    Michigan's Children*, 153
Alum Rock School District, 63
American Civil Liberties Union (ACLU),
    123
Armed Forces, U. S., 50
Arnof, Dorothy, 36-38
Atlanta, Ga., case study of organizing in,
    136-139, 140
Atlantic Monthly, 1-2
Attribute theories, 16

Back of the Yards Neighborhood
    Council, 77, 123
Bailey, Robert, Jr., 107-108
Ballenger, B., 108
Berger, Eugenia H., 116-117
Berger, P. L., 111
Berube, M. R., 50, 78
Betts, R., 31
Bilingual Education Act, 88
Blaming the Victim (Ryan), 17
Blaming-the-victim hypothesis, 2
Borman, Kathryn, 15, 40, 49
Boston, Mass., case studies of organizing
    in, 136-139, 140
Boston's School Committee, 133
Boyer, Ernest L., 40, 47-48
Boyte, H., 2
Bradbury, Katherine L., 5
Bronx Committee Project, 80
Brown, F., 69, 95

Brown decision, 41-42, 81, 82-83
Bryan, W. L., 111
Buffalo Board of Education, 96
BUILD Academy, 69, 95-96, 138, 146
Bureaucracy, 70-76
Burgherside, Ogbu's study on, 19-24

Callahan, R., 39, 54
Carver High School, 121
Central cities, definition of, 8-9
Central High School, 83
Chestnut Heights Association (CHA),
    43-44
Child advocacy groups, 92
Christopher Gibson School, 133-134
Chung, Norman H., 94, 99
Cincotta, G., 102
Citizen advisory councils, 90-92
Citizen groups, building consensus in,
    149-150
Citizen participation, 1. *See also*
    Organizing, organizations
    forerunners of, 4, 70-81
    liberal legacy of, 4, 82-101
    in multi-issue neighborhood
        organizations, 102-115
    school desegregation and, 82-86
Civic Clubs of Houston, 79-80
Civilian Conservation Corps (CCC),
    76
Civil Rights Act of 1964, 83
Clark, Reginald, 25-27
Classrooms
    ineffective instruction and, 36-39
    inner-city, 29-39
    teacher culture shock and, 30-34
Cloward, Richard A., 64
Cohen, Wilbur, 90

Comer, James P., 3, 64–69
Communist Party of the United States of
    America (CPUSA), 77
Communities. *See also* Organizing,
    organizations
  citizen participation in education and,
    76–78, 82, 86, 94–100
  neighborhoods compared with, 10–13
  school reform models and, 52–53, 55,
    64–66, 69
  shift away from organizations in,
    11–13
  theoretical forms of school linkage
    with, 119–128
Community Development Block Grant
    (CDBG) program, 103, 114
Community School Boards (CSBs),
    98–99
Comprehensive Employment and
    Training Act (CETA), 103
Conference of Mayors, 103
Congress of Racial Equality (CORE),
    133
Coombs, Jerrold R., 49
Cooper, H. M., 34
Crowfoot, J., 84–85
Crystal City school system, 93–94
Cuban, L., 49
Cubberly, Ellwood P., 72
Culture-of-poverty hypothesis, 2, 16
Culture shock, 30–34
Cunningham, J. V., 108
Curriculum
  citizen participation in education and, 74
  neighborhood/school organizational
    linkages and, 125, 128
  reform of, 52–53, 66, 81
  victimhood and, 21–22
Cusick, P. A., 36

Dahl, Robert, 140
Davies, Don, 80, 84, 91, 93, 95, 99, 113,
    117–118
Davis, Bertha, 36–38
*Death at an Early Age: The Destruction
    of the Hearts and Minds of Negro
    Children in the Boston Public
    Schools* (Kozol), 133
Demerell, Reginald G., 1
Detroit public schools, 42, 99, 100

Discipline, organizing on issue of,
    155–158
Discrimination, 43–45
Downs, Anthony, 5, 9

Eastown Community Association (ECA),
    140–141, 147
Economic Opportunity Act, 103
Edmonds, Ron, 82, 130, 148
Education
  for all handicapped children, 89–90
  citizen participation in. *See* Citizen
    participation
  compensatory, 86–88
  complexity of, 3, 29–50
  meanings of parent/citizen
    involvement in, 116–119
  multicultural, 88–89
Educational Consolidation and
    Improvement Act (ECIA), 87
Education Department, U. S., 88
Education for All Handicapped Children
    Act, 89
Effective schools research, school reform
    and, 46–50
Eisenstadt, Thomas, 133
Elementary and Secondary Education
    Act (ESEA), 83, 87, 90
Emergency School Aid Act (ESAA), 87
English as a Second Language (ESL),
    program, 21
Equal Educational Opportunities, Survey
    (Coleman Report), 42

Federal Aid Highway Act, 79
Federal Home Loan Bank Act, 79
Felt, M. C., 46
Fish, J. H., 139–140
Fisher, R., 73–74, 80
Flint Community School Program, 79
Fogarino, S., 112
Follow Through, 119
Foster, Car, 95
Foster, Herbert L., 32–33, 35
Fragmentation, 18–19
Froman, R. D., 51
Fulton Elementary School, 75–76

GI Bill, 81
Gittell, Marilyn, 132, 136–139

Goetze, R., 7
Good, T. L., 34
Grace, G., 17
Greenstein, J., 158
Gross, N., 80
Guitierrez, Jose Angel, 93–94
Guthrie, J. W., 42

Hallman, H. W., 2
Hammond, Ray, 24, 27
Handicapped children, 89–90
Hatton, B., 74, 79
Havighurst, R. J., 99
Head Start, Project, 21–22, 50, 87, 119
Health, Education, and Welfare (HEW)
    Department, U. S., 83, 90
Heights Community Congress, 84
Hersh, R., 40, 48, 51, 69, 146
Highland Community School, 98
Homework, 159
Howard, Jeff, 24, 27
How to Change the Schools: A Parents'
    Action Handbook on How to Fight
    the System (Lurie), 156, 157
How to Fix What's Wrong with Our
    Schools (Davis & Arnof), 36
Hughes, Langston, 133
Hull House, 74

Individually Guided Education (IGE),
    52–58
Industrial Areas Foundation, 108
Inner cities, definition of, 8–9
Inner-city public schools. *See also*
    Schools
    failures of, 1–2, 29–50
    federal initiatives for improvement
        of, 86–92
Institute for Responsive Learning,
    117
Instruction, ineffective, 36–39
Instructional Programming Model
    (IPM), 53

Jackson, Jesse, 27
Jacobson, Lenore, 34
James, R., 103
Jim Crow laws, 25
Joyce, Bruce R., 3, 40, 48, 51, 69, 146
Justice Department, U. S., 94

Kahn, R. L., 40, 112–113
Kahn, S., 129
Karp, W., 51
Katz, D., 40, 112–113
Katz, Michael B., 71, 75
Kelly, Edward Joseph, 123
Kerner Commission Report, 90
Kettl, D. F., 103
King, Martin Luther, Jr., 36–37
King, Samuel, 72
King-Baldwin School Project, 64, 66–67,
    117–118
Klausmeier, Herbert J., 52
Kohl, Herb, 49
Kozol, Jonathan, 133–134

Labov, W., 162
Lamb, Curt, 14, 107–108
Lancourt, Joan, 106, 109
LaNoue, G., 80
Lantner, P., 95
Lau v. Nichols, 88
League of Cities, 103
Learned helplessness, 24
Learning, high-order, basic skills vs.,
    36–39
Lee, Barrett A., 11–13
Leff, L., 108
Leighton, B., 10
Lemann, Nicholas, 1–2
Levin, H. M., 29
Levine, D. U., 48, 81, 85, 87, 89, 153, 160
Lightfoot, Sara L., 121
Limits of Citizen Participation: The
    Decline of Community
    Organizations (Gittell), 136–139
Litwak, Eugene, 116, 119–130
Local education agencies (LEAs), 90
Los Angeles public schools, 99–100
    case study of organizing in, 136–139,
        140
Lukas, J., 133
Lurie, Ellen, 132, 156–160

McCune-Nicolich, L., 162
McKibbin, M., 40, 48, 51, 69, 146
Mann, Horace, 54, 70–71
Marciniak, E., 79
Mayer, N. S., 115
Meier, A., 73, 75

Mexican American Youth Organization
(MAYO), 93–94
Meyer, Henry, 116, 119–130
Miller, Z. L., 10
Milliken v. Bradley, 100
Milwaukee's Federation of Independent
Community Schools, 97
Model Cities legislation, 103
Morris, R. S., 7
Moscow, H., 51
Mott Community School Plan, 74
C. S. Mott Foundation, 74, 78–79, 91
Multi-issue neighborhood organizations,
102–115
goals, structure, issues and norms of,
109–111
influence of federal initiatives on,
103–104
leadership of, 106–109
as mediating institution, 111–113
as vehicle for school reform, 113–115
*Myth of Educational Reform: A Study of
School Responses to a Program of
Change, The* (Popkewitz,
Tabachnick & Wehlage), 57

Nader, Ralph, 104
Naison, M., 77
National Association for the
Advancement of Colored People
(NAACP), 80, 82–83, 123, 128
National Coalition of Advocates for
Students, 154–155
National Coalition of ESEA Title I
Parents, 91
National Defense Education Act, 81
*Nation at Risk: The Imperative for
Educational Reform, A*, 46
Neighborhood Guild, 73–74
Neighborhoods
case study of discrimination in
organizing in, 43–45
changes in organizations of, 11–13
determinants of political styles of,
141–146
distressed, as context for organizing,
8–13
exploring linkages between schools
and, 4, 116–131, 146–147

multi-issue organizations of, 102–115
as political concept, 9–11
poor, resident attitudes toward schools
in, 3, 15–28
reassessing decline of, 1–14
sources of decline of, 2, 5–8
types of, 9
withdrawal of capital from, 5–8
Neighborhood Youth Corps, 103
Neuhaus, R. J., 111
New York Board of Education, 80
New York City public schools, 1, 158
decentralization of, 62–63, 98–99, 100
New York Free School Society, 71
Nix, H., 106

Office of Civil Rights, 42
Office of Education, 91
Ogbu, John, 19–23, 25–26
Opportunity theory, 16
Organization for a Better Austin (OBA),
108
Organizing, organizations. *See also*
Citizen participation
case study of discrimination in, 43–45
from community to neighborhood,
11–13
despair and, 136–139
distressed neighborhoods as context
for, 8–13
lessons from case studies of, 132–147
multi-issue. *See* Multi-issue
neighborhood organizations
for neighborhood school improvement
campaigns, 154–161
of parental anger, 132–135
radical, 76–79
setting goals for, 139–141
social work approach to, 78
*Organizing for Family and
Congregation*, 108
Ornstein, A. C., 48, 81, 85, 87, 89, 153,
160
Orr, E. W., 37
O'Shea, D., 100
Owen, S. V., 51

Parent advisory committees (PACs),
91–92

Parents
  case studies of organizing and,
    132–135, 141–142, 144, 146–147
  failures of inner-city public schools
    and, 29–30, 39–40, 42–45, 49–50
  in interaction with children, 25–27
  meanings of educational involvement
    of, 116–119
  neighborhood school improvement
    campaigns and, 148–152, 154–155,
    159–161, 163
  organizing and anger of, 132–135
  participation in education of, 70, 73,
    89–99
  school reform models and, 55, 59–60,
    62–69
  victimhood and, 15, 19–23, 25–27
Parents' Guide: Measuring Your School's
  Expectations, 155
Parent-teacher conferences, 159–160
Payne, Charles M., 16, 18, 22, 24, 29, 31,
  33
Perlman, Janice E., 105–106
Peters, Thomas J., 3, 58–59, 61–62
Piven, Frances Fox, 64
Playboy, 123
Popkewitz, T. S., 52–54, 57
Portland public schools,
  bureaucratization of, 72–73
Public Citizen, 104
Public Education Associations, 62, 80
Public Law (PL) 89–750, 90
Public Law (PL) 91–230, 90–91
Public Law (PL) 93–380, 89, 91
Purkey, S. C., 40, 48
*Pygmalion in the Classroom: Teacher
  Expectation and Pupils' Intellectual
  Development* (Rosenthal &
  Jacobson), 34

Racial Ethnic Parent Council (REPC), 84
Ravitch, Diane, 61, 83, 98
Raza Unida Party, 93–94
Reagan, Ronald, 7, 103
Redneck-as-Patsy (RAP) thesis, 17
Rehabilitation Act, 89
Report cards, 160
*Report of the National Advisory
  Commission on Civil Disorders*, 5

Restore Our Alienated Rights (ROAR),
  84
Rich, J. M., 46
Rich, R. C., 108
Rockefeller Foundation, 91
Rogers, David, 94, 99
Roosevelt, Franklin Delano, 76
Roosevelt Community School, 95
Rosenbaum, Patricia L., 9
Rosenfeld, Gerry, 30–31
Rosenthal, Robert, 34
Rudwick, E., 73, 75
Rural Electrification Administration, 76
Ryan, William, 17

Sarason, Seymour B., 36, 41, 58
Schoenberg, Sandra P., 9
School-as-Community-Center movement,
  14, 73–75, 78–79
School reform, 2, 3
  case studies of neighborhood
    organizing for, 4, 132–147
  effective schools research and, 46–50
  excellent corporation model of, 51–52
  multi-issue neighborhood organizations
    as vehicles for, 113–115
  packaged innovation model of, 51,
    52–58
  partnership model of, 52, 62–64
  responsible party model of, 69
  third-party model of, 52, 64–67
Schools. *See also* Inner-city public
  schools
  attitudes of poor toward, 3,
    15–28
  bottom-up community control and
    decentralization of, 92–100
  bureaucracy in governing of, 70–76
  case study on breakdown of, 19–24
  citizen participation in. *See* Citizen
    participation
  desegregation of, 82–86
  determinants of neighborhood political
    style and, 141–146
  on district and state level, 152–154
  inequities in funding of, 41–43
  linkages between neighborhoods and,
    4, 116–131, 146–147
  machine model of, 39–41, 43

Schools. (*continued*)
  mounting campaigns for improvement
    of, 4, 148–164
  observing and gathering data on,
    150–154
  parent/child interaction and, 25–27
  residents' deference for, 144
  successful, 161–163
  as systems, 39–45
  teacher culture shock and, 31–34
  victimhood and, 15, 18–24
Seattle, Wash., 11–13
Seeley, David S., 3, 39, 62–65
Servicemen's Readjustmant Act, 79
Settlement House movement, 14, 73–75,
    78–79
Sieber, R. Timothy, 43
Sigsbee Park Elementary School,
    140–141
Skills, 36–39
Small, Kenneth A., 5
Smith, B., 80
Smith, M. S., 40, 48
Smith-Hughes Act, 76, 80
South Arsenal Neighborhood
    Development (SAND) Everywhere
    School, 97
Spring, Joel, 15, 40, 49, 75
Stachura, Edward, 133–134
Starr, Ellen Gates, 74
Students
  case studies of organizing and,
    133–135, 140–142, 144
  citizen participation in education and,
    71, 74, 83–85, 87–90, 93–101
  failures of inner-city public schools
    and, 29–48, 50
  in interaction with parents, 25–27
  neighborhood school improvement
    campaigns and, 148–163
  neighborhood/school organizational
    linkages and, 116–121, 124–125, 127,
    130
  as school operations participants,
    160–161
  school reform models and, 52–67
  teacher culture shock and, 30–34
  teacher expectation and achievement
    of, 34–36
  victimhood and, 15–16, 18–27

Sullivan, Marguerite, 133
Summerfield, Harry L., 116, 121, 126,
    129, 141–146
Supreme Court, U. S., 80–81, 82–83, 88

Tabachnick, B. R., 52–54, 57
Taylor, Frederick, 39
Teacher evaluation, 158–159
Teachers
  case studies on organizing and,
    133–135, 141–142, 144, 146–147
  citizen participation in education and,
    71, 75, 86–88, 95–101
  culture shock experienced by, 30–34
  failures of inner-city public schools
    and, 29–45, 48
  neighborhood school improvement
    campaigns and, 148–152, 154–160,
    162–163
  neighborhood/school organizational
    linkages and, 124–125, 129–130
  school reform models and, 52–58,
    60–62, 64–69
  student achievement and expectations
    of, 34–36
  victimhood and, 18–20, 22–25
Testing, school reform and, 48–49
Tofani, L., 133
Toynbee Hall, 73
Tyack, D., 71–72

United Community Defense Service
    (UCDS), 80
United Community Services (United
    Fund), 97, 114
United Federation of Teachers, 99

Victimhood, 15–28
Violas, Paul, 75–76
Voluntarism, 70–72
Volunteers in Service to America
    (VISTAs), 103

Wagner Act, 76
War on Poverty, 103
Warren, D., 9
Warren, R., 9
Waterman, Robert H., Jr., 3, 58–59,
    61–62
Wayland, S., 74

Webb, Rodman, 24
Weber, Max, 18, 39
Wehlage, G., 52–54, 57
Weinberg, Meyer, 41–42, 70, 85–86, 88, 91, 93, 119
Wellman, B., 10
Westminster Neighborhood Association School, 100
Westside High School, 24, 33
Williams, Michael R., 2, 11, 104, 111–112, 140
Winner, L., 7

Wisdom, John Minor, 83
Woodlawn Association, The (TWO), 73, 110, 139–140
Woodlawn Experimental Schools Project (WESP), 139–140
Woodlawn Improvement Association, 73
Woolfolk, A. E., 162

Yale University, Child Study Center of, 64, 66–67, 117–118
Young, Coleman, 99

About the Author

Michael R. Williams is Professor-in-the-College at Aquinas College, Grand Rapids, Michigan. He has taught undergraduate courses in education, general studies, philosophy, and urban studies. He received the Licentiate in Philosophy (Ph.L.) from St. Louis University in 1966, the Master of Science in Mechanical Engineering (M.S.M.E.) from Marquette University in 1970, and the Ph.D. in urban education from the University of Wisconsin-Milwaukee in 1974. After teaching in the Milwaukee Public School System, he was the cofounder and first administrator of the Highland Community School in Milwaukee. He has been a neighborhood activist in Grand Rapids since 1974 and is the author of *Neighborhood Organizations: Seeds of a New Urban Life*.